YOUR
Signature
MOVE

MASTER YOUR MINDSET
MAXIMIZE YOUR PRESENCE
AND MULTIPLY YOUR IMPACT

DR. DEYONNE PARKER

Your Signature Move:
Master Your Mindset, Maximize Your Presence, and Multiply Your Impact

For permissions or inquiries, visit
www.DeYonneParker.com

Published by: Dr. DeYonne LLC.
ISBN: 979-8-9995297-0-1
Printed in the United States of America
Book cover design: Lavon Lewis, Creative Velocity Agency
Interior layout: Muhammad Harris
Editor: Ethleen Sawyerr, Speak Write Play

Disclaimer:

This book is intended for informational and inspirational purposes only. While every effort has been made to ensure accuracy, the author and publisher assume no responsibility for errors or omissions. The strategies and tools presented are based on personal experience, professional coaching insight, and research. Readers are encouraged to apply them with discernment and seek professional guidance as needed.

All trademarks and brand names mentioned are the property of their respective owners.

First Edition: 2025

DEDICATION

To every woman who dared to ask, "Is there more for me?" This book was written with you in mind. To the mentors, sponsors, and truth-tellers who lifted me, and to the women and men I've been honored to coach, mentor, develop, and lead. **Thank you for your trust, your brilliance, and your bravery.**

TABLE OF CONTENTS

INTRODUCTION

THE POWER OF YOUR SIGNATURE MOVE

So, What Is a Signature Move?

I'm so glad you asked! Picture a chessboard, not just as a game, but as a metaphor for life, leadership, and legacy. On that board, no piece carries more power, versatility, and influence than the Queen. She's not confined to limited paths—she moves boldly in any direction. She doesn't just react to the moves of others—she sets the tone, commands the board, and reshapes the outcome of the game with strategy and strength.

That's the essence of *Your Signature Move*. It's the way you show up, lead, and influence with distinction. It's not random or reactive. It's purposeful. It's your refined, practiced, and unforgettable strength. A powerful combination of skill, talent, character, and expertise that sets you apart and positions you to move with intention and impact.

Every one of us possesses a unique power, a personal strategy forged from lived experiences, perspective, and values. And yet, too often, we hesitate, shrink, or second-guess our right to step into our full potential. This book is your invitation to stop waiting and start moving.

As a multi-faceted woman navigating leadership across the corporate world, ministry, and entrepreneurship, I've wrestled with the challenge of mastering my mindset; making bold, strategic moves; and effectively communicating my value. For years (and I do mean *years*), I questioned if I was qualified to lead in unfamiliar rooms, if I could truly make an impact or if it was ok for me to want more.

I've experienced the weight of self-doubt, the fear of stepping into bigger opportunities, and the complexity of juggling multiple callings. I've navigated toxic leaders, career pivots, and moments that chipped away at my confidence. But through deep work, prayer, strategy, and intentional action, I found that my ability to rise was rooted in my ability to own my position on the board, trust my moves, and make them boldly.

That's what Your Signature Move is all about: stepping into your Queen-level strength with clarity, confidence, and courage.

Through years of growth and transformation, I discovered mine: **I am a Courage Catalyst.**

I activate boldness in others. I lead with vision and heart, igniting confidence, sparking clarity, and inspiring courageous action. My Signature Move is empowering others to rise, take risks, and step into what they were called to do with courageous intent.

With 20+ years in global learning and leadership development, I've coached, mentored, and trained professionals across industries who were leading teams, making pivots, or trying to define their next bold move. And here's what I've learned: your Signature Move doesn't just elevate your career—it transforms how you show up in every space you step into.

I've helped many people break free from their comfort zones, stop playing small, reclaim their voice, and discover their Signature Move. Now, it's your turn.

The Signature M.O.V.E.™ Framework

Just like a master chess strategy, your next level requires intentional thinking and powerful execution. That's where the Signature M.O.V.E.™ Framework comes in. It's your playbook for discovering and activating your Queen-like influence through four key moves:

M

MASTER YOUR MINDSET

Your thoughts shape your reality. You'll learn to silence self-doubt, embrace confidence, and shape a leadership mindset that grounds every move.

O

OWN YOUR PRESENCE & PERSONAL BRAND

Whether in a boardroom, on a stage, or in everyday interactions, your presence matters. You'll learn to build credibility, communicate with purpose, and make your presence unforgettable in every room you enter. You belong.

V

VENTURE WITH INTENTION

Queens don't move aimlessly. Learn to make strategic career decisions, embrace high-value opportunities, and take bold steps that align with your values and goals.

E

EXPAND YOUR IMPACT

It's not just about personal success— your moves make space for others. Discover how to mentor, network, and create opportunities for others with legacy in mind.

Each section of this book is anchored in the Signature M.O.V.E.™ Framework, offering practical strategies, coaching insights, guided exercises, and real-world examples to deepen your understanding and help you put your Signature Move into action.

What Can You Expect from This Book?

I wrote this book for the woman who knows she's capable of more but just needs a framework and some fire to go after it. If that's you, know that I see you. I've been you. And now, I'm cheering for you.

This book is not just theory—it is the wisdom gained from my own professional journey and the experiences of other dynamic women who have stepped into their Signature Move. Each chapter in this book combines practical strategies, relevant examples, and actionable exercises to help you implement the Signature M.O.V.E.™ Framework in your own life.

You'll learn how to:

- ♟ Build unshakable confidence and step into your next level or opportunity with authority.
- ♟ Overcome common career roadblocks and take ownership of your growth.
- ♟ Leverage relationships and networks to create meaningful opportunities.
- ♟ Develop a personal brand that aligns with your strengths and values.
- ♟ Make decisions that position you for long-term success.
- ♟ Utilize your talent and experiences to mentor and lift others.

Additional Questions You Might Be Asking

1. **Is this book only for women, or can men benefit from it too?**

   Absolutely! While this book was written with women in mind, the principles of confidence, leadership, and strategic action apply to anyone. If you want to strengthen your professional presence, advance your career, or step boldly into opportunities, the strategies in this book will serve you well, regardless of gender.

This Book Is for You If...

- ❑ You've questioned your potential or hesitated to take the next step in your journey.
- ❑ You're an aspiring or established leader ready to elevate your career.
- ❑ You're a ministry leader or entrepreneur ready to grow and overcome self-doubt and fear
- ❑ You want to step into greater confidence and command attention in your field.
- ❑ You are tired of waiting for opportunities and ready to create your own.
- ❑ You believe that leadership is about impact, influence, and leaving a legacy.
- ❑ You know you have more to offer and are ready to make your Signature Move.

2. Is this book <u>only</u> for people in formal leadership roles?

Not at all! *Your Signature Move* is for anyone who wants to lead, grow, and thrive—whether in a corporate setting, entrepreneurship, ministry, or personal leadership. Leadership is not about a title—it's about influence, confidence, and action. This book will help you step into those things, no matter where you are.

3. Will this book help me if I'm an entrepreneur or in ministry leadership?

Absolutely! Whether you're building a business, leading a ministry, or navigating a corporate career, the principles in this book apply. Your ability to master your mindset, own your presence, make strategic decisions, and expand your impact are keys to success in any leadership or career path.

4. Will this book help me if I struggle with self-doubt and imposter syndrome?

Yes! Many brilliant, capable women second-guess themselves, hold back from speaking up, or feel like they're not "qualified enough" for the opportunities they want. This book will help you break free from limiting beliefs, build unshakable confidence, and step boldly into the spaces you belong in.

5. What if I don't know what my Signature Move is yet?

That's exactly why this book exists! You'll gain clarity on your unique strengths, talents, and professional presence through reflection exercises, real-world case studies and the M.O.V.E.™ Framework. By the end of the book, you'll not only have an idea of what your Signature Move is, but you'll also know how to activate and maximize it.

6. If I already know what my Signature Move is, can this book still help me?

Absolutely! Just like a master chess player returns to familiar strategies to sharpen them, there's always room to refine your Signature Move. Even if you already know your most powerful move, this book will help you reposition it, expand its reach, and elevate your impact. Great players don't just rely on what they know—they study, practice, and evolve to stay one step ahead.

Your Signature Move will help you strengthen how you lead, communicate, and influence—especially when the stakes are high. It's not just about knowing your move; it's about knowing when and how to use it with clarity, confidence, and courage. Growth is a lifelong game—and this book ensures you keep playing with strategy.

7. Will this book help me if I feel stuck in my career?

Great question! This book will help you get clear on what you want, build confidence in your strengths, and become bold enough to jump into your courage zone—whether that's a promotion, career pivot, business venture, or leadership role.

8. How is this book different from other leadership or career advice books?

Unlike traditional leadership or career advice books that focus solely on strategies, *Your Signature Move* combines mindset mastery, confidence building, and actionable career growth strategies into one transformative guide. It's not just about professional advancement—it's about becoming the most powerful version of yourself.

Let's Get Started!

This is an interactive journey, so grab a pen to highlight key insights. Mark the margins with your thoughts and work through the exercises. You can read this book straight through or jump to sections that resonate most with your current season. Most importantly, apply what you learn. Transformation happens when you take action!

This is your moment to embrace the tools, mindset, and strategies that will propel you to your next level. No more waiting. No more shrinking. The time is now! Let's M.O.V.E.™

ON THE FOLLOWING PAGES, YOU'LL FIND YOUR FIRST EXERCISE
DESIGNED TO HELP YOU DISCOVER YOUR SIGNATURE MOVE.

Exercise: Discovering Your Signature Move

The exercise below is designed to help you define your unique value, the way you lead and influence, and the message you want to leave behind—all wrapped up into your own Signature Move. Even if you already know your Signature Move, this exercise will help you refine, expand, and take it to the next level.

NOTE: If you find yourself struggling to answer any of the questions below, keep moving through the book and come back to this exercise. The insights you learn on the following pages might just unlock the answers you need to discover your Signature Move.

STEP 1:

REFLECT ON YOUR STRENGTHS AND SUPERPOWERS

♟ What do people consistently come to me for?

_____

_____

_____

♟ What do I do effortlessly that others find difficult?

_____

_____

_____

♟ What energizes me most when I'm helping others?

_____

_____

_____

♟ What are my top three strengths or talents?

_____

_____

_____

♟ What are my top three values?

_____

_____

_____

♟ In moments when I've truly felt "in my zone," what was I doing?

_____

_____

_____

Write down 3–5 key words or phrases that capture your essence (e.g., strategist, encourager, connector, truth-teller, builder, visionary).

♟ _____

♟ _____

♟ _____

♟ _____

♟ _____

STEP 2:

DESCRIBE YOUR POWER AND IMPACT

Choose a phrase or single word that best reflects the power and impact you show up with when you're at your best.

Examples: Boldness Builder, Strategy Whisperer, Legacy Leader, Vision Architect

Formula: *[Adjective or Power Word] + [Impact Word or Identity]*

List a few below and circle your top choice:

♟ _____

♟ _____

♟ _____

♟ _____

♟ _____

♟ _____

STEP 3:

CRAFT YOUR PERSONAL DEFINITION

Answer this prompt to create a one-paragraph personal definition of your Signature Move:

When I'm operating in my Signature Move, I_____.

Template (Use this as a guide):

A (power word + impact word) *is someone who ____. She helps others ____, leads by ____, and is known for ____. Her presence creates ____, and her purpose is to ____.*

STEP 4:

WRITE YOUR TAGLINE

Now, craft a short, powerful statement that captures your Signature Move. This is your declaration.

Template Examples:

- ♟ *"I help others [verb], [verb], and [verb]. I am a [Signature Move]."*

- ♟ *"I don't just [what you do]—I [impact you create]."*

- ♟ "I lead with [value], live with [value], and move with [value]."

📝 Examples:

- ♟ ***Dr. Dee's tagline:*** *"I am the hand on your back pushing you out of your comfort zone and into your courage zone. I am a Courage Catalyst."*

- ♟ "I lead with purpose, connect with heart, and build with vision. I am a Legacy Leader."

Optional: Use AI to Help You Refine Your Signature Move

Not sure how to put it all into words? Try using an AI tool (any tool you're comfortable with) to support your process.

Here are a few **prompts you can try**:

- ♟ "Based on these words [insert your strengths or key traits], what would be a powerful Signature Move title for me?"

- ♟ "Help me write a personal definition of my Signature Move: [insert your chosen phrase or one-word title]."

- ♟ "Can you give me tagline options for someone who is known for (insert power + impact words)"
- ♟ "Help me describe how I use [insert top strengths] to influence and lead others."

 PRO TIP:

AI shouldn't replace your voice—it's purpose is to help you find the words when you feel stuck. Use it as a creative partner to help unlock your thoughts.

Gentle Reminder:

You don't need to have it all figured out today. The goals are clarity and intention. Your Signature Move may evolve over time, but today, you're taking ownership of the way you were designed to lead, influence, and impact.

OWN IT. DECLARE IT. LIVE IT.

NOTES

01

MASTER YOUR MINDSET

BREAK THROUGH LIMITING
BELIEFS AND STEP INTO YOUR
POWER

CHAPTER

MINDSET MATTERS IN LEADERSHIP AND SUCCESS

You've likely heard phrases like "mind over matter," "stinking thinking won't get you anywhere," or "your thoughts dictate your actions." Whether they resonate with you now or have echoed through past experiences, these words hold undeniable truth: Your mindset shapes your reality and is the foundation of everything you do. Every move you make (or don't make) starts in your mind. Whether you're applying for a promotion, launching a business, or stepping into a new leadership role, your mindset will either accelerate your success or hold you back.

The way you think about yourself, your abilities, and your opportunities directly impacts how you show up. If you believe you're capable, deserving, and equipped, you will act accordingly. If you doubt your worth, hesitate to take bold steps, or allow fear to dictate your decisions, you will stay stuck (believe me, I know).

In this chapter, you're going to discover the power of your mindset and deal head-on with the challenges causing you to cast doubt on your capabilities.

Mastering your mindset is the first and most critical step in discovering, owning, and executing your Signature Move. Why? Because if you don't believe you're skilled and capable enough for the next level you want to achieve, who else will? Right? Right!

Rethinking Leadership: Not Just a Title

Before we dive deeper, let's first shift our thinking and break limiting beliefs around the word *leadership*, as this word will appear throughout the book and serve as one of the guiding principles for our journey. When most people hear the word *leadership*, they immediately think of executives, managers, or people with formal authority. But leadership is not just about a title. It's about the ability to influence, inspire, and create impact wherever you are.

True leadership is demonstrated in everyday moments: taking initiative in a project, mentoring or coaching a peer, making a strategic decision, or advocating for an idea. It's about stepping into your personal power and showing up with clarity, confidence, courage, and conviction, regardless of whether you have an official leadership title.

Think about the most influential people in your life. Were they always your boss? Probably not. Instead, they were people who led with vision, spoke with conviction, and inspired action in the workplace, in their community, or among their friends and family.

My First Leader

The first leader I ever knew was my mother, Mrs. Carol Jean Harvey. She wasn't a CEO (though she earned that title in our home with her repeated phrase, "I pay the cost to be the boss!"). She didn't have a formal leadership position, and no one handed her a title. But she led our household with resilience, wisdom, and strength (and she would let you know who paid the rent at the address we occupied). As a single parent, she made hard choices that required courage and a whole lot of prayer every day!

I watched her navigate financial struggles, career transition challenges, and the responsibility of raising a family on her own. She showed me that leadership wasn't about a title after my signature or nameplate on a desk. It was about standing firm in who I am, making bold decisions even when they're difficult, and never settling for less than what I deserve.

She taught me that leadership was about knowing my worth, advocating for myself and others, and having the courage to keep moving forward, even in the face of adversity. Through my mother, I learned that true leaders don't wait for permission—they step into their power and create opportunities where none seem to exist. Her example shaped the way I see leadership today, and it continues to inspire me to lead with confidence and courage to embrace my Signature Move!

So, even if you are not in a leadership role today, developing leadership skills is a game-changer for your career. They allow you to stand out, create opportunities, and position yourself for growth, whether that means a promotion, a new career path, or greater professional impact.

- ♙ Take initiative and solve problems
- ♙ Communicate effectively and inspire others
- ♙ Think strategically and make informed decisions
- ♙ Adapt to change and embrace challenges
- ♙ Demonstrate confidence and leadership presence

The exercises that follow are designed to help you recognize your current leadership strengths and value. Jump in and get started. Your AHA moments are waiting for you.

Exercise: Your Influence Inventory

This exercise will help you recognize and own the ways you already lead (formally or informally) and identify areas where you can deepen your influence in both your personal and professional environments.

Instructions: Set aside 20–30 minutes of quiet, uninterrupted time for this reflective exercise. Grab your journal or open a blank document on your device and work through the questions thoughtfully. Be honest, curious, and open—this is about discovery, not judgment.

PART 1:

RETHINKING LEADERSHIP

Reflect on the following:

1. How do you define leadership in your own words?
   (Example: "Leadership is showing up, taking initiative, and inspiring others to act.")
2. Who are influential leaders in your life or career? What qualities do these people embody?
3. Do you believe you need a title to lead? Why or why not?

PART 2:

WHERE DO YOU ALREADY LEAD?

List the spaces and situations where you currently demonstrate leadership or influence, no matter how big or small. Use the prompts below to guide you.

At Work:

♜ Do you take initiative on projects or contribute innovative ideas?

♜ Have colleagues sought your guidance, feedback, or support?

♜ Have you ever mediated conflict, supported team morale, or advocated for others?

In Your Community or Personal Life:

♜ Do you lead in your family, faith-based organization, or volunteer work?

♜ Do people come to you for advice, encouragement, or direction?

♜ Are you the go-to person in any particular area (planning, organizing, motivating)?

Write down at least five ways you currently lead, even if you've never labeled them as leadership positions before.

1. _____
2. _____
3. _____
4. _____
5. _____

PART 3:

WHAT IS YOUR INFLUENCE STYLE?

Reflect on your natural style of influence.

1. When you're at your best, how do you influence others (through listening, taking action, teaching, setting an example, using persuasion, demonstrating empathy, executing strategy, etc.)?

2. What is your signature strength as a leader or influencer?

3. Where do you tend to hold back, and what beliefs may be limiting your influence?

PART 4:

EXPANDING YOUR INFLUENCE

Use the following prompts to think about how you can grow your leadership impact:

1. What's one area in your work or life where you'd like to lead more boldly?
2. Who do you need to influence or advocate for more intentionally?
3. What would it look like to show up more confidently in that space?
4. What mindset shifts would support this next level of influence?

Action Step:

Write one powerful, personal leadership intention statement that captures how you want to lead going forward.

Dr. Dee's Example:

I lead with heart and vision, igniting confidence, sparking clarity, and inspiring courageous action. I empower others to rise, take risks, and step into what they were called to do with impact and intention.

CHAPTER

BREAKING LIMITING BELIEFS & BUILDING BOUNDARIES

Now that we've cleansed our lenses to see leadership in a different light, it's time to tackle and tame our self-doubt and overly critical inner voice. They've been running rampant for far too long, so it's time to crush these confidence killers.

Self-doubt, imposter syndrome, fear of visibility...Wow...the struggle is real! You know what I mean, the little voice inside that whispers, What if I fail? Am I really qualified? Do I belong in this room? These thoughts drain us emotionally, mentally, and physically. Even more exhausting is the facade we wear as we pretend to have it all together while hiding the struggles we pray no one sees.

The Invisible Chains of Self-Doubt

Limiting beliefs (or "dirty talk" as I like to call them) are like invisible chains that hold us back from stepping into our full potential. These deeply ingrained thoughts—*I'm not good enough, I don't have what it takes, and success isn't meant for me*—shape the way we see ourselves and the opportunities around us. The danger of these beliefs is that they don't just live in our minds; they dictate our actions. When we believe we are unworthy of success, we hesitate, shrink, or settle for less. But here's the truth: The only thing standing between where you are and where you want to be is the belief that you belong there. (Boom! Now, that is a truth bomb.)

So, how did we get so far away from the truth?

Challenging the Lies You've Accepted as Truth

Our minds are filled with narratives—some empowering, others destructive. The most dangerous lies are the ones we don't even realize we've accepted as truth. Many of the limiting beliefs we carry didn't originate with us. They were planted through past experiences, societal expectations, childhood conditioning, or the words of others. Perhaps you were told that leadership wasn't for you, that speaking up meant being "too much," or that failure was proof you weren't capable. Over time, these lies became internalized, shaping the way you showed up in the world. But just because a thought has lived in your mind for years doesn't mean it deserves a permanent place. These are mere stories you tell yourself, and stories can be rewritten!

The first step to breaking free is interrogation: questioning these beliefs with the same scrutiny you would apply to a misleading headline. Ask yourself, Who told me this? Is this belief serving or limiting me? What would I do if I no longer carried this thought? When you begin to see these lies for what they are, false narratives that have kept you playing small, you reclaim the power to rewrite your story. Replacing these limiting beliefs with empowering truths isn't just a mental exercise. It is an act of self-liberation. The moment you challenge the lie, you weaken its hold and loosen its grip on you.

Reframing the Narrative

The next step is reframing. Breaking free from limiting beliefs isn't just about letting go of negative thoughts. It's about replacing them with empowering truths.

What if, instead of doubting your abilities, you started affirming your potential?

Reframing self-limiting beliefs doesn't mean ignoring your challenges. It means shifting how you see them, from something that holds you back to something that opens new possibilities.

Think about the difference between saying, "I'm not ready" and "I'm learning and growing every day." One keeps the door closed. The other opens it.

When you stop seeing rejection as failure and start viewing it as redirection, you build resilience.

Reframing your mindset helps you see challenges as stepping stones, not roadblocks. And as you start to change the story you tell yourself, you begin to rewrite your reality by turning doubt into confidence and hesitation into bold action.

Navigating Challenging and Toxic People

Your mindset isn't just shaped by your own thoughts. It's also shaped by the people around you.

Let's be real, some folks are just draining. Whether it's a co-worker, a boss, a friend, or even a family member, their energy can weigh you down. They might plant little seeds of doubt, question your decisions, or make you second-guess your worth. Sound like anyone you know? (If they're sitting near you, just smile and keep reading.)

That's why protecting your mindset means paying attention to who gets access to your energy.

I love what media personality Porsha Fox says: "Make your haters your motivators." Instead of letting toxic people throw you off track, let their doubt push you to go even harder. Let their negativity remind you why you're moving forward in the first place.

The stronger your mindset becomes, the less power those people have over your peace, your progress, or your purpose.

Toxic people don't all look the same. They show up in different ways, and knowing what kind of energy you're dealing with can help you handle it better.

Before you label someone toxic, do a quick gut check: Is this a pattern or a bad day? What is the impact on you? Have you clearly set a boundary yet? If the behavior is repeated, draining, and resistant to feedback, you are likely dealing with toxic energy. Here is how it often shows up and what you can do.

Credit Taker

✒ **Profile:** The Credit Taker claims your ideas or work as their own or blurs ownership when it is time to be recognized.

⚙ How They Operate:

- Present your deliverables without giving you credit.
- Switch to "we" language after you do the heavy lift.
- Delay or block opportunities for you to share your work directly.

◎ Their Impact on You:

- You question whether advocating for yourself is worth the friction.
- Key stakeholders or sponsors do not see your true impact.
- Motivation drops because recognition feels unsafe.

✋ How to Handle Them:

- Move to written records: "For clarity, I led A and B. Jordan led C."
- Ask to present your work: "I will walk the team through the approach and results."
- Loop in leaders early with brief status notes that show authorship.

Chronic Complainers

Profile: The Chronic Complainer is never satisfied and ALWAYS finds something to be negative about. Whether it's work, leadership, opportunities, or personal challenges, they dwell on feelings of frustration and spread pessimism.

How They Operate:

- They constantly highlight problems but never offer solutions.
- They drain your energy by venting endlessly about the same issues.
- They encourage group negativity by getting others to join in their misery.

Their Impact on You:

- Lowers morale and makes environments feel toxic.
- Can make you second-guess positive experiences because of their perspective.
- Wastes time and emotional energy that could be spent on progress.

How to Handle Them:

- Set boundaries—limit how much time you engage with their negativity.
- Shift the conversation and say, "I hear your frustration. What are some possible solutions you can come up with?"
- Detach emotionally—their complaints are not your responsibility to fix.

Underminers

Profile: The Underminer operates with passive-aggressive tactics to subtly question your competence, devalue your contributions, or sow doubt among your peers. They are skilled at making side comments, planting seeds of doubt, and diminishing your confidence without being overtly aggressive.

⚙ How They Operate:

- ♟ They give backhanded compliments: "Oh, you did well...for someone new to this."
- ♟ They avoid giving you credit for your ideas or subtly diminish your success
- ♟ They create an undercurrent of doubt about your leadership, skills, or decisions.

◎ Their Impact on You:

- ♟ Can erode your self-confidence over time.
- ♟ Makes you feel like you're constantly proving yourself.
- ♟ Creates a tense, distrustful environment.

☞ How to Handle Them:

- ♟ Call out the behavior professionally but directly by saying, "It sounds like you're questioning my decision. Can you clarify?"
- ♟ Keep your receipts—document your contributions so there's no room for doubt.
- ♟ Build strong alliances—when others recognize your value, Underminers lose power.

Manipulators

🖋 **Profile:** The Manipulator is a master of control, often using guilt, deception, or emotional tactics to get their way. They twist narratives, make you feel obligated, and always have an agenda that benefits them.

⚙ How They Operate:

- ♟ They twist words or situations to their advantage.
- ♟ They use guilt trips to get you to do things that serve them.
- ♟ They make you feel responsible for their needs, workload, or emotions.

⚙ Their Impact on You:

- ♟ Can make you feel drained and obligated without realizing it.
- ♟ Causes self-doubt by making you question if you're being unfair.
- ♟ Creates imbalanced relationships where they always benefit.

⚙ How to Handle Them:

- ♟ Set firm boundaries—say "no" without over-explaining.
- ♟ Recognize emotional manipulation tactics and detach.
- ♟ Don't negotiate with guilt. Their emotions are not your responsibility.

Dream-Crushers

🔖 **Profile:** The Dream-Crusher thrives on dismissing, minimizing, or discouraging others' ambitions. They rarely see possibility—only limitations, risks, and reasons why things won't work.

⚙ How They Operate:

- ♟ They shoot down ideas before they can even take shape.
- ♟ They use phrases like "that's unrealistic," "that's not how things work around here," or "I don't see that working at all. You might want to think of something else."
- ♟ They often mask negativity as "just being realistic or keeping it real" or "playing devil's advocate."

⚙ Their Impact on You:

- ♟ Kills creativity and makes you question your own potential.
- ♟ Creates self-doubt before you even take action.
- ♟ Reinforces fear of failure instead of possibility.

How to Handle Them:

- Don't seek their validation. Your dreams don't need their approval.
- Respond with confidence and say, "I believe in this, and I'm moving forward."
- Surround yourself with Dream-Builders, not Dream-Crushers.

Gaslighters

Profile: The Gaslighter is the most psychologically manipulative of the group. They twist reality, make you question your own experiences, and distort the truth to make themselves look right and you feel unstable.

How They Operate:

- Deny reality by saying, "That never happened" or "You're imagining things." They never admit fault.
- Twist facts to make you doubt your memory or perception.
- Play the victim and make you feel guilty for questioning them.

Their Impact on You:

- Causes self-doubt and confusion to make you wonder if you're overreacting.
- Creates emotional exhaustion so that you feel the need to defend yourself constantly.
- Can isolate you from others by making you feel like the problem.

How to Handle Them:

- Trust your experiences. Don't let them rewrite your reality.
- Keep written records of conversations and agreements.
- Call them out with facts, not emotions, and say, "Actually, we discussed this last week, and you said…"

Navigating challenging and toxic people can leave emotional residue that lingers long after the interaction ends. That's why learning how to protect your energy and peace is more than just a self-care practice—it's a leadership imperative. Because the truth is, you can't pour from an empty cup, and you certainly can't thrive from a place of depletion. Let's explore how to set powerful boundaries, preserve your peace, and stay grounded in environments that may try to knock you off balance.

Protecting Your Energy & Peace

You have the right to protect your peace.

At some point in your journey, you realize that protecting your peace isn't just a nice idea, it's a necessity. The more you grow, the more intentional you'll need to be about who and what you let into your space. That includes your mind, your energy, and your spirit.

Start paying attention to how you feel after certain conversations. Do you leave feeling seen, supported, and inspired? Or do you feel small, second-guessed, or completely drained? Those feelings are clues.

If someone constantly makes you question your worth, your instincts, or your direction, that's not just "how they are." That's a signal. And it's time to create a plan to protect yourself.

Boundaries are not walls, they're filters. They help you make room for what aligns with your purpose, your peace, and your vision for the future. And here's the truth: not everyone deserves full access to you.

Toxic people feed off your reaction. They thrive on confusion, drama, and the energy they can pull from you. Whether it's someone who constantly criticizes, manipulates, or just can't celebrate your growth, the goal is the same, keep you small. But that's not your story anymore.

Now ask yourself: What has it cost you to tolerate chaos disguised as loyalty? What have you sacrificed by shrinking, appeasing, or constantly walking on eggshells? How much longer are you willing to delay your peace just to maintain a false sense of harmony?

You deserve relationships that energize you, spaces that support you, and boundaries that protect the version of you that's still becoming.

You've come too far and worked too hard to let someone else's chaos throw you off course. So protect your peace like your purpose depends on it—because it does.

Here are some quick reminders for building your boundaries:

- ☑ **Limit Exposure:** Reduce time spent with those who negatively impact your mindset. Not every person deserves unlimited access to you (learn this lesson now!).
- ☑ **Redirect the Conversation:** If negativity dominates discussions, shift the dialogue to something constructive or excuse yourself.
- ☑ **Stand Firm in Your Confidence:** When others project their fears or insecurities onto you, remind yourself that their limitations are not yours to carry.
- ☑ **Seek Supportive Spaces:** Surround yourself with people who encourage your growth, celebrate your wins, and challenge you in healthy ways.

"There is no power without peace. And there is no peace without boundaries."

DR. DEYONNE PARKER

CHAPTER

03

MINDSET MASTERY IN ACTION

Mindset mastery doesn't happen in a vacuum—it's lived out in real-world challenges, decisions, and defining moments. The following case studies are drawn from real scenarios experienced by a small subset of the women I've had the honor to coach and mentor over the course of my career. While their names have been changed for privacy, their journeys are authentic and deeply powerful. Each one reveals what mindset mastery truly looks like and reminds us that transformation begins the moment we stop believing the lies and start standing in our truth.

Real-Life Examples

Case Study #1: From Dimmed Down to Dialed Up

Maya's Story

Maya was a mid-level manager in a corporate firm. She had great ideas but rarely spoke up in meetings, fearing that she wasn't experienced enough. She watched colleagues—some less qualified—get promoted, while she stayed stagnant. The turning point? I challenged her to track every time someone valued her input. Within a month, she realized that her voice was respected, but she was the one holding herself back.

Maya made three key mindset shifts:

- ☑ She stopped seeking perfection before speaking up.
- ☑ She embraced discomfort, knowing growth happens outside of comfort zones.
- ☑ She redefined failure as feedback.

Within six months, Maya led a major project, and within a year, she was promoted. Her skills didn't change—her mindset did!

Case Study #2: Leading Beyond the Title

Jasmine's Story

Jasmine, a talented young professional, was selected to lead a high-visibility project involving senior executives—an incredible opportunity that triggered overwhelming self-doubt. Without an official leadership title, she struggled with imposter syndrome, questioning if she was truly qualified or simply being taken advantage of. Was she in over her head, or was she being strategically positioned for growth? The weight of that uncertainty made her hesitate, second-guessing every decision she made.

Her breakthrough came when I asked her one simple question: "If you weren't capable, would they have trusted you with this opportunity?"

That question forced Jasmine to shift her mindset.

- ☑ She began to see that her skills, ideas, and contributions had earned her a seat at the table.
- ☑ She reminded herself that leaders are not defined by titles but by the ability to bring vision, strategy, and results to the table.

☑ Instead of shrinking in the presence of executives, she owned her expertise, asked thoughtful questions, and confidently presented solutions.

By the end of the project, not only had she gained the respect of senior leaders, but she also proved to herself that she was ready for more. Jasmine's leadership was not about a title—it was about stepping up, speaking up, and delivering impact.

Case Study #3: Rebuilding Confidence After a Toxic Leader

Aaliyah's Story

Aaliyah was a high-performing professional with a track record of excellence. But after being assigned to a new manager with a harsh, critical leadership style, she began to second-guess herself. Her leader rarely acknowledged her contributions, frequently criticized her work in front of others, and made subtle remarks that chipped away at Aaliyah's confidence. At first, Aaliyah tried harder, thinking she needed to prove herself. But over time, the constant negativity began to erode her self-esteem, leaving her anxious and unsure of her own abilities.

It wasn't until we had a candid conversation that Aaliyah realized she wasn't imagining things; she was experiencing emotional toxicity, and it was impacting her mindset. With support and coaching, she began to rebuild her confidence by documenting her accomplishments, seeking feedback from trusted peers, and challenging the false narratives she had internalized.

Aaliyah also made a strategic decision to advocate for herself, requesting a role shift to a different department where her skills were needed and appreciated. In her new environment, she flourished, leading key initiatives and rediscovering her voice. Aaliyah's story is a reminder that no title or toxic leader has the right to diminish your worth—it highlights the importance of recognizing emotional toxicity, rebuilding self-belief, and reclaiming power through mindset and support.

The mindset breakthroughs you just read? They're not just inspiring—they're proof. Proof that real transformation isn't just for a select few. It's available to any woman who's ready to do the inner work. These stories show what's possible when you start challenging the old beliefs, rebuilding your confidence, and choosing to move forward on purpose.

And while everyday women are out here rewriting their stories in bold and beautiful ways, there's also a lot we can learn from women at the top—the leaders, visionaries, and game-changers. These are the women who've faced real challenges, owned their power, and shown us what it truly means to lead with clarity, confidence, and courage.

Let's dive into some of their mindset lessons. You might just find your next breakthrough in their story.

Lessons from High-Achieving Women

Throughout history, great women have transformed their industries, careers, and communities by mastering their mindsets. Their stories reveal how resilience, confidence, and intentional thinking can turn setbacks into stepping stones and aspirations into achievements. Allow me to shine a light on a select few.

Serena Williams silenced critics with an unshakable confidence in her abilities and a trailblazing record that redefined what excellence looks like—not just in women's tennis, but in the world of sports. Competing in a space often dominated by male narratives and underestimated expectations, she shattered records with 23 Grand Slam singles titles, the most by any player in the Open Era. Her relentless pursuit of greatness, fierce presence on the court, and unapologetic authenticity off it have cemented her legacy as not only one of the greatest tennis players of all time, but as a cultural icon of power, resilience, and possibility.

MINDSET LESSON:

Own your space—fully and unapologetically. Confidence isn't about arrogance; it's about knowing your worth, trusting your preparation, and showing up with the mindset that you belong at the top of your game.

Indra Nooyi, the former CEO of PepsiCo, shattered barriers in a male-dominated industry by maintaining a mindset of resilience and strategic thinking. When she was doubted, she didn't shrink but used challenges as fuel to push forward instead. Her mindset of continuous learning and adaptability positioned her as a powerhouse in corporate leadership.

 MINDSET LESSON:

Don't shrink to fit the room—stretch to shape it. Let every challenge sharpen your vision and expand your capacity.

Consider also **Sara Blakely**, founder of Spanx. She turned rejection into redirection by refusing to let setbacks discourage her. Her belief in herself, despite being repeatedly told "no," led her to build a billion-dollar empire from scratch.

 MINDSET LESSON:

Rejection isn't the end—it's a redirection. When doors close, your belief can build new ones.

Dr. Maya Angelou—world-renowned poet, bestselling author of I Know Why the Caged Bird Sings, civil rights activist, and one of the most influential voices of our time—openly wrestled with imposter syndrome. Yes, even someone with her brilliance and legacy questioned her worth. In one candid moment, she shared:

"Each time I write a book, every time I face that yellow pad, the challenge is so great. I have written eleven books, but each time I think, 'Uh oh, they're going to find out now. I've run a game on everybody and they're going to find me out.'"

 MINDSET LESSON:

Doubt doesn't disqualify you. You can feel fear and still show up fully. Your worth isn't erased by insecurity—it's revealed through your resilience.

Another powerhouse is **Senior Pastor Sarah Jakes Roberts**, who turned personal challenges into a powerful platform for transformation. Once weighed down by self-doubt and public scrutiny for being a teenage mother, she refused to let her past define her. Through faith, resilience, and a mindset shift, she reclaimed her purpose, becoming a renowned speaker and leader who inspires millions through her global ministry and bestselling book *Woman Evolve*.

 MINDSET LESSON:

Your past may shape you, but it doesn't define you. Healing begins when you believe that your broken pieces can build something beautiful.

Lastly, another powerful lesson comes from **Sheryl Sandberg, former COO of Meta**, who once shared that women often hold themselves back by waiting until they feel 100% qualified before going for an opportunity. She illuminated the confidence gap and challenged women everywhere to take the leap before they feel fully ready.

A widely cited internal report by Hewlett-Packard revealed that men will often apply for a job when they meet just 60% of the qualifications, while women tend to wait until they meet 100%. This confidence gap was later highlighted in The Confidence Code by Katty Kay and Claire Shipman (2014), sparking global conversations about how self-belief—not just skill—often determines who rises.

MINDSET LESSON:

You don't have to feel 100% qualified to show up powerfully. Progress is made by those who dare to say "yes" before they have all the answers.

Ketanji Brown Jackson, the first Black woman to serve on the U.S. Supreme Court, exemplifies the power of perseverance and presence. Despite years of scrutiny and underestimation, she remained grounded, prepared, and unapologetically poised. Her mindset was not shaped by the noise around her, but by the clarity within her. She stayed ready, so she never had to get ready.

 MINDSET LESSON:

Preparation is power. When you know who you are and what you bring to the table, no room can silence your impact.

These powerful legacy stories remind us that mindset isn't just a buzzword—it's the foundation for every bold move we make. Whether navigating imposter syndrome, reclaiming purpose, or stepping into opportunity before feeling fully prepared, the common thread is a shift in thinking. And that shift doesn't happen by accident. It's a daily, intentional process—one that begins within.

Now that you've seen what's possible, it's time to turn inward and do the work. In this next chapter, we'll explore how to challenge your inner critic and embrace a new mental blueprint—your mental makeover—designed to support the woman you are becoming.

NOTES

CHAPTER

YOUR MENTAL MAKEOVER

Your mindset is either your greatest asset or your biggest obstacle. Too often, we unknowingly operate under false beliefs, mindset myths that keep us playing small, second-guessing our potential, and stuck in fear. As I stated earlier in this section, just because you've believed something for years doesn't make it a fact.

Years ago, I came across a quote that changed my perspective: "Doubt and fear kill more dreams than failure ever will." Those words hit me deeply, making me realize that I wasn't being held back by external obstacles. No, I was imprisoning myself with fear. That quote became a wake-up call, helping me see how much power I had been giving to doubt instead of believing in my own potential.

I knew something had to change. If doubt and fear were capable of holding me back, then confidence and courage had to be the key to moving me forward.

Confidence is your currency. The inner wealth that frees you from limiting beliefs and equips you to lead, speak, and show up with intention. Confidence isn't just a feeling, it's actually a skill that can be developed, strengthened, and refined over time. Yet, many of us hesitate, second-guess ourselves, or play small because we haven't taken the time to truly assess where our confidence stands and what's holding us back. It's not about being perfect. It's about choosing to believe in your worth even when doubt tries to take the lead.

When you tap into your confidence, you unlock your Signature Move. So, yes, my friend, it's time to serve an eviction notice to those thoughts that have lived rent-free in your head and give yourself a mental makeover!

I don't know about you, but I love a good makeover because it leaves me feeling refreshed, renewed, and like a whole new woman. But this time, the transformation isn't about how you look. It's about how you think. This mental makeover will empower you to replace fear with confidence, uncertainty with clarity, and doubt with the courage to step fully into your Signature Move.

To begin your mental makeover, consider the following mindset missteps and strategies for overcoming them. Pay particularly close attention to those that you are struggling with right now and start building out your personal strategy to overcome them.

Mindset Missteps

1. Fear of Failure

The fear of failure often leads to the avoidance of taking big leaps or risks. But failure is not the opposite of success, it's part of the journey. Every failure holds a lesson, and those who embrace setbacks as learning opportunities develop resilience and wisdom.

How to Overcome It:

- Shift from thinking, *What if I fail?* to *What will I learn if this doesn't work?*
- Reframe failure as feedback, not a final verdict.
- Create a failure résumé and identify key lessons you've learned.
- Celebrate small wins to build confidence over time.

2. Perfectionism & Overthinking

Where are my perfectionists? Perfectionism keeps many of us stuck in the cycle of "almost ready." The truth? You will never feel 100% ready. There will always be something to fix, change, or make better. Done is better than perfect. Growth comes from taking action, even before you feel fully confident.

How to Overcome It:

- Replace thinking, *It needs to be perfect* with *I need to start* or *I need to finish*.
- Set deadlines for decisions to avoid analysis paralysis.
- Accept that mistakes are part of learning and growth.
- Find an accountability partner to push you when you get stuck in perfectionism (This has truly helped me!).

3. Fear of Visibility

Fear of visibility is more than just shyness—it's the hesitation to be fully seen, heard, and recognized for who you are and what you bring to the table. It's the voice that whispers, "What if I'm not good enough? What if they judge me? What if I fail in front of everyone?" This fear keeps many women playing small, staying silent in meetings, downplaying their achievements, or avoiding opportunities that require them to step into the spotlight. But the truth is, your voice, presence, and perspective matter—and the world can't benefit from what you have to offer if you're too afraid to show up. Visibility isn't about perfection—it's about owning your space (more on this later).

How to Overcome It:

- Take a presentation course or join a public speaking club.
- List moments when your voice made a difference.
- Find a coach or mentor to support and challenge you.
- Say "yes" to an opportunity that scares but stretches you.

Your Breakthrough Begins Now

Mastering your mindset doesn't mean you never experience doubt—it means you don't let doubt stop you. It's time to challenge your old beliefs, embrace your potential, and step into a mindset that supports the meaningful moves you are destined to make.

The most powerful thing you can do today is decide that your limiting beliefs no longer define you. You are not your past mistakes, your doubts, or the expectations others have placed on you. You have the power to rewrite your story, step into your full potential, and pursue your dreams without hesitation. The breakthrough you've been waiting for starts with one decision: believe in yourself more than you believe in your fears.

The most successful women are not those who never experienced doubt or struggles with their mindset—they are the ones who pushed through it and showed up anyway. Let's choose differently. Let's break free from doubt, fear, and limiting beliefs to step boldly into the truth of who we are!

Top Ten Takeaways

A strong mindset isn't something you develop once and then forget. It's a daily practice!

Here's how you can cultivate it:

1. **Affirmations & Self-Talk:** Speak positively about yourself and your abilities.
2. **Continuous Learning:** Invest in books, courses, coaches, and mentors who challenge your thinking.
3. **Surround Yourself with Growth-Oriented People:** The right environment will push you to think bigger and take action.

4. **Take Small, Bold Actions Daily:** Confidence and courage are built through action, not waiting until you "feel" ready.

5. **Reframe Failure as Feedback:** Every setback is a lesson in disguise. Instead of fearing failure, use it as fuel for growth and improvement.

6. **Clarify Your Vision:** Clearly define what success looks like for you—having a strong "why" will keep you motivated through challenges.

7. **Embrace Discomfort:** Growth happens outside your comfort zone. Lean into discomfort as a sign that you're stretching into your full potential.

8. **Own Your Value:** Stop downplaying your skills and accomplishments. Advocate for yourself, communicate your worth, and step into rooms with confidence.

9. **Protect Your Peace:** Set boundaries that support your goals and well-being. Say "no" to distractions, negativity, and anything that doesn't align with your purpose.

10. **Practice Gratitude and Celebrate Progress**: Acknowledge how far you've come. Gratitude grounds you, and celebrating your growth—big or small— builds momentum and reinforces a mindset of possibility.

You've just taken in ten powerful insights—now it's time to apply them. Awareness is the first step, but real transformation happens when you pause, reflect, and put intention into action. Let's shift from learning to aligning. The next few pages are designed to help you check in with where you are, what you need, and what boundaries or beliefs might need to shift so you can move forward with confidence.

Start by exploring your Confidence Compass—then use the Energy Check & Boundary Builder to clarify what's fueling you, what's draining you, and how to protect the space you need to shine.

Exercise: The Confidence Compass

The Confidence Compass is designed to help you pinpoint where you are, recognize what's fueling or hindering your self-belief, and chart a path toward greater confidence. By the end of this exercise, you'll gain clarity on where you need to grow, how to silence self-doubt, and what steps will help you step into your next level with certainty. This is your moment to get real, get clear, and get confident!

Your Signature Move begins with how you think about yourself. Let's M.O.V.E.™!

Instructions:

Take a moment to reflect on your strengths and areas needing growth. Answer the following questions:

♜ What three things do I excel at?

_____

_____

_____

♜ When have I been recognized for my work or leadership?

_____

_____

_____

♜ What fears or doubts are holding me back?

_____

_____

_____

♟ What doubts do I need to reframe into empowering beliefs?

_____

_____

_____

Deeper Reflection: What's Holding You Back?

Take a moment to reflect on the following questions. Be honest with yourself. Your answers to these questions will help uncover the mindset blocks you need to address.

♟ Do I fear success as much as I fear failure?

_____

_____

_____

♟ Am I shrinking myself in certain situations?

_____

_____

_____

♟ What would I do if I knew I couldn't fail?

_____

_____

_____

Exercise: Energy Check + Boundary Builder

PART 1:

ENERGY CHECK – WHAT'S FUELING YOU VS. DRAINING YOU?

Every time you say "yes" to what drains you, you're saying "no" to what fuels your purpose. Invest your "YES" wisely and exercise your "NO" boldly. This is your invitation to check in, reset, live, and lead from a place of strength, not depletion.

This exercise is meant to raise awareness of the people, tasks, environments, and habits that impact your energy, mindset, and ability to lead and thrive.

Read through and respond to the following questions.

1. What fuels and energizes me?

Write down specific people, activities, spaces, or moments that give you energy, make you feel inspired, or help you feel grounded and powerful.

Examples:

- ♟ Creative brainstorming sessions
- ♟ Conversations with growth-minded friends
- ♟ Time in prayer or meditation
- ♟ Clear plans or structure

2. What drains or depletes me?

List the people, patterns, responsibilities, or environments that leave you feeling heavy, anxious, exhausted, or disconnected.

Examples:

- ♟ Overcommitting
- ♟ People-pleasing

- ♖ Unclear boundaries
- ♖ Toxic coworkers or unsupportive leaders

PART 2:

BOUNDARY BUILDER – RECLAIMING YOUR POWER

This next section will help you identify where boundaries are needed and create intentional practices to protect your time, energy, and peace.

Reflection Prompts:

1. Where in my life am I saying "yes" when I really mean "no"?
2. What obligations or relationships feel one-sided or emotionally draining?
3. What conversations am I avoiding that could help restore balance?
4. What boundary would give me space to rest, think, or lead more powerfully?

Boundary Builder Template:

Use this structure to name your boundary, why it matters, and how you'll uphold it.

I will no longer _____
because it is costing me _____.

I will start _____.
And I will communicate this by _____.

Example:

I will no longer **accept last-minute meetings during my focus time** because it is costing me **clarity and productivity.**

I will start **blocking off non-negotiable focus hours.**
And I will communicate this by **updating my calendar and letting my team know.**

PART

02

OWN YOUR PRESENCE & PERSONAL BRAND

SHOW UP. BE SEEN. BE FELT.

05

PRESENCE SPEAKS LOUDER THAN WORDS

Think about your favorite brand. What makes you loyal to it? What makes you recommend it to others without hesitation? Chances are, it's not just the logo or product, it's the experience. Maybe it makes your life easier, makes you feel seen, or consistently delivers value that exceeds your expectations. That brand leaves an impression on you.

Now flip it. If you've ever had a negative experience with a brand, poor service, lack of integrity, broken promises, you probably didn't hesitate to share that story either. Why? Because how something or someone makes you feel lingers long after the interaction is over.

The same is true for you.

Whether you realize it or not, you are a brand, and it's not just your résumé, elevator pitch, LinkedIn profile, or Instagram bio. It's the felt experience people have with you, the impression you leave long after the meeting ends, the tone you set when you speak, and the energy you bring into every space you enter. That impression is shaped by your presence.

Your presence is more than just how you walk into a room. It's the real-time expression of who you are and what you stand for.

It's your voice, your values, and your vibe all working together. When the way you carry yourself, speak up, and show up aligns with what you believe and what you bring to the table, that's when people start to take notice. That's when your presence starts speaking for you, even before you say a word.

The truth is, your personal brand isn't just built on resumes and bios. It's built in the everyday moments, how you make people feel, the energy you bring, and the consistency they can count on.

So ask yourself: When you walk into a space, what are you radiating? Because whether you realize it or not, your presence is either reinforcing your brand or rewriting it.

Every interaction you have is a moment of impact. So, the question becomes:

How do you want people to describe you when you're not in the room? What do you want them to say about how you make them feel, how you show up, or what you contribute?

Owning your presence is about showing up with intentionality and clarity, knowing who you are and what you bring to the table, and being unapologetic about both. You don't have to be the loudest person in the room to have presence, you just have to be the most aligned. Let me say that again: Presence isn't about volume. It's about alignment.

It's easy to assume that people who speak the most, gesture the biggest, or walk in with booming energy are the ones who own the room. But some of the most powerful professionals and leaders I've encountered weren't the ones talking the loudest, they were the ones who were anchored in who they were.

You don't have to fight for attention. You command respect because you're rooted in your identity and moving with purpose, not because you demand it.

Alignment means you're present, not performing. You're not shrinking to make others feel comfortable, and you're not inflating yourself to impress. You're simply showing up fully as yourself, and that is what makes your presence unforgettable.

So, if you've ever thought, *I'm too quiet to lead* or *I don't have the personality to take up space, hear me clearly.* You don't need a louder voice; you need a stronger connection to your truth. And when you speak from that place, you won't just be seen—you'll be felt.

Whether you're leading a team, interviewing for a new role, launching your business, or speaking on a stage, how you show up can command attention, earn trust, and leave a lasting impression. But only if you own it.

Owning your presence is a decision. A decision to stop shrinking. A decision to stop second-guessing. A decision to show up fully, speak boldly, and lead with unwavering clarity.

My Truth

I haven't always felt like I belonged in the rooms I walked into.

Early in my career (and even in some moments of leadership) I often battled the feeling that I didn't belong, like my voice didn't carry the same weight as others at the table. Full of ideas, I sat quietly because I was afraid to speak up for fear of saying the wrong thing. I found myself shrinking, second-guessing, and overthinking how I came across, especially in rooms filled with people who had titles, years of experience, and global influence.

When I was given the opportunity to travel internationally to coach and develop global leaders, my first instinct was to turn it down. I stood at the edge of one of the biggest opportunities of my career—and almost walked away because of uncertainty. I questioned whether I was the "right fit," was "qualified enough," had a presence that would be respected. But something shifted. I knew I couldn't keep dimming my light because of fear. So, I made the decision to own my presence by becoming clear on who I already was, not pretending to be someone else.

It didn't happen overnight. I had to practice. I started preparing more intentionally, speaking up even when my voice trembled, and reminding myself that I was invited into these spaces for a reason. Over time, I realized that presence isn't about perfection—it's about alignment. The more I led from a place of authenticity and clarity, the more confident I became. I wasn't just occupying space—I was owning it.

SOUND FAMILIAR?

HOW DOES MY TRUTH RESONATE WITH YOURS?

Mini Coaching Moment:

Ask yourself the following questions. Take a moment to reflect and respond.

♟ "Where in my life am I turning down my presence to fit in, and what would it look like to show up fully aligned with who I truly am?"

_____

_____

_____

♟ What would shift in the room if I stopped shrinking?

_____

_____

♟ What would become possible if I brought my full self to the table?

_____

_____

Lead with Presence (Even Without the Title)

We've been conditioned to believe that leadership starts when we get a title. But the truth is, influence doesn't begin with a role. It starts with how you carry yourself.

Your presence can shift dynamics, build trust, and create momentum long before your name appears on the org chart. Leadership is more than a position—it's a posture. And people are always watching how you walk in it.

Your presence opens doors before you walk through them. It earns respect before a promotion is offered. It builds credibility before the job title catches up.

So, if you're waiting for the title to finally give yourself permission to lead, stop. You already are. Start owning your presence now, not someday. Because presence doesn't just reflect who you are—it shapes who you become.

In the next chapter, we'll explore six facets that will help shape your presence.

NOTES

_____

_____

_____

_____

_____

_____

_____

_____

_____

_____

_____

_____

_____

_____

_____

_____

_____

_____

_____

_____

_____

_____

_____

_____

_____

_____

THE 6 C'S OF PRESENCE

As I shared in the previous chapter, presence is more than posture, polish, or projection. It's the energy you carry, the clarity you hold, and the impact you make without saying a word. It's how you show up when no one announces you and how people experience you long after you've left the room.

That's why I'm sharing with you the **6 C's of Presence**: simple, yet powerful, reminders to help you develop and elevate how you walk into rooms, lead conversations, and represent your values with conviction. Whether you're navigating a boardroom, pulpit, pitch meeting, or virtual call, these six qualities will help you show up as the most aligned, powerful version of yourself—consistently and unapologetically. Let's dive in and begin putting them in action.

The 6 C's of Presence

1. ◈ **Clarity** – Be clear on who you are, what you value, and the message you want to communicate.

Clarity is the foundation of presence. When you know your values, your voice, and your vision, you're less likely to get thrown off course by comparison, insecurity, or chaos around you. Clarity helps you enter a room already grounded in purpose—so you're focused even if you're nervous. The clearer you are internally, the stronger you show up externally.

Ask yourself:
- ❑ What do I want to be known for?
- ❑ What energy do I want to bring into this space?

2. 🧘 **Composure** – Stay grounded and calm under pressure. Your steadiness becomes your strength.

Composure is your ability to remain present, centered, and unshaken, even when tension rises or the spotlight is on you. It doesn't mean you won't feel nervous—it means you don't let that nervousness take over. People trust those who can stay steady. Your calm presence can shift the temperature of an entire room.

Practical tip:
Take a deep breath, drop your shoulders, and pause before you speak. That moment of stillness resets your power.

3. 🗣 **Conciseness** – Communicate with intention. Less is more when your message is clear and powerful.

Powerful presence isn't about saying more—it's about saying what matters. Rambling or over-explaining dilutes your message. Conciseness reflects confidence, clarity, and preparation. When you speak, people listen because they know you're not wasting words.

Practice this:
Before a meeting or conversation, jot down 1–2 key points you want to make. Then, deliver them with focus and intention. Remember, fewer, better words.

4. ✦ **Confidence** – Speak and carry yourself with self-assurance, even when you feel nervous. Confidence is built through action.

   Confidence grows when you take bold action, follow through, and show up for yourself. It's in your posture, your tone, your eye contact, and your willingness to own your brilliance—even when you feel shaky inside.

   Affirmation:
   "I am qualified. I am enough. I deserve to be in this room."

5. ⚷ **Courage** – Push through discomfort. Say what needs to be said. Show up even when it feels risky.

   Courage is the decision to show up even when you feel afraid. It's pressing "unmute" when your voice is shaking. It's raising your hand when you're unsure of the outcome. It's leaning into growth when hiding feels safer. You don't have to feel courageous to be courageous. Every act of courage builds the kind of presence that moves people.

   Ask yourself:
   If I weren't afraid, what would I say or do in this moment?
   Then, take a small bold step in that direction.

6. ⚑ **Credibility** – Know your stuff! Own your experience and back it up with preparation and consistency.

   People respect what is rooted in preparation and integrity. Credibility is built by consistently showing up, doing the work, and delivering excellence. It doesn't require perfection—it requires ownership. You are your own best advocate when you can clearly articulate your value and back it up with results.

   Reminder:
   Simply put, ABC - Always Build Credibility. You've earned your seat. Now, own it.

Your presence isn't just about how you look. It's about how people experience you. It's the energy you bring, the confidence in your voice, and the calm you carry, even when things get tense.

When you show up with clarity, confidence, courage, and credibility, you're not just filling space, you're owning it with intention. And when you stay composed and speak with purpose, people remember you for the right reasons.

Here's the thing: those six C's? You don't have to chase them. They're already in you. You activate them by choosing to show up fully, without shrinking.

So, next time you step into a room, remember, your presence doesn't need permission or applause. It just needs you to walk in and own it.

Before we go any further, I want to share a real coaching story with you about a client who struggled with being concise when it mattered most.

As you read her story, think about your own. What parts hit home for you? What might you need to shift in how you show up?

Coaching Case Study:
Helping a Leader Communicate with Clarity

Client: "Monica"
Role: Senior Director at a global consulting firm
Challenge: Struggled to get to the point in high-stakes meetings. While her updates were thoughtful and thorough, they often overwhelmed the audience with too much detail. Her message would sometimes get lost and so would the opportunity to influence.

Session Focus:
Monica and I uncovered that her over-explaining came from a desire to prove she had

done the work and "earned the room." She feared that simplifying her message might make her seem unprepared. I posed a new question: **"What if being concise isn't about saying less, but more about making what you say count?"**

Together, we focused on the power of brevity, practicing how to turn complex updates into clear, compelling talking points using a simple structure: **Context → Key Point → Call to Action.** I also introduced the concept of the "Executive Minute"—how to deliver value in 60 seconds or less.

Transformation:
In just a few weeks, Monica began receiving stronger feedback from leadership. One senior executive told her, "You've really sharpened the delivery of your presentations." Monica shared, "I realized I don't need to say everything to be seen as effective. Clear is powerful."

She now leads executive briefings with precision and is frequently tapped to present key updates to leadership.

Reflection Questions:

- Where in my communication do I tend to over-explain—and why?
- What limiting belief drives my need to prove or over-justify?
- What message do I need to deliver this week—and how can I make it more clear and compelling?
- How might fewer, focused words increase my influence?

Monica's story reveals something powerful: influence isn't just about having something to say—it's about how effectively you say it. Mastering your message is one part of the equation, but how you carry that message is what elevates it. And this leads us to a deeper conversation that many professionals overlook: the distinction between being seen and truly being felt. That's where the difference between visibility and presence comes into play.

Visibility vs. Presence: Be Seen *and* Felt

Let's be real: In today's hyperconnected world, it's easier than ever to be visible. You can have a polished LinkedIn profile, rack up likes on Instagram, show up in all the right rooms, and still walk away feeling unseen.

That's because visibility isn't the same as presence.

According to a 2024 Harvard Business Review study, nearly 58% of professionals report feeling overlooked or undervalued in the workplace, even when they're highly visible in meetings and projects. Visibility may get your face in the feed or your name on the invite list, but presence is what makes people pay attention.

So what's the difference?

- ♜ Visibility is about being noticed. It's external—your activity, your exposure, your online footprint.

- ♜ Presence is about being felt. It's internal—your energy, your clarity, your ability to command attention without demanding it.

You can be on stage and still not be heard. You can speak up in meetings and still not be taken seriously. But presence? Presence shifts the atmosphere. It's when your words land, your confidence speaks louder than your credentials, and your character is the part people remember most.

And presence isn't about perfection. It's about alignment. When your mindset, message, and movement are working together, people feel that. Presence is built when you walk into a space and people sense your intention before you say a word.

Think of it like this:
Visibility gets you in the room. Presence makes the room remember you.
And in a world full of noise, presence is your superpower.
So here's your question: Are you just showing up... or are you standing out?

Let's Further Explore the Difference

In the chart below you can see the subtle yet significant difference between being visible and being truly present—and why mastering presence is your real power move.

👁 VISIBILITY	🧭 PRESENCE
Being in the room	Owning your space in the room
Getting attention	Creating connection and credibility
Showing up physically	Showing up energetically and intentionally
Surface-level recognition	Deep, lasting impact
Often external or image-focused	Always internal and value-aligned

So, yes—be visible. Raise your hand. Apply for the opportunity. Step into the light. But also develop the inner alignment that allows your presence to speak before you say a word.

NOTES

CHAPTER

WHAT'S SHRINKING YOUR SHINE?

Now that we've explored the difference between simply being seen and truly being felt, it's time to go deeper. Because even with the desire to stand in our full power, many of us unknowingly dim our own light. Whether it's fear, perfectionism, comparison, or people-pleasing—something is often working behind the scenes to shrink our shine. If you've ever felt invisible despite showing up, or found yourself second-guessing your brilliance, this chapter is for you.

Even the most brilliant women can unintentionally shrink in rooms where they should be shining. Whether it's fear, conditioning, or past experiences, we all carry internal patterns that try to mute our presence. These "presence pitfalls" are subtle, but they can have a big impact on how we show up and are received.

Let's explore a few common pitfalls and ways to reframe them:

1. Shrinking to Fit In

"If I say too much, I'll sound like I'm bragging..."

You dilute your voice to avoid being "too much" or "too loud." But shrinking doesn't make you more humble—it makes you invisible. You were not created to play small.

☑ **Reframe:** "My voice adds value. I can shine and still make space for others."

2. Over-Apologizing

"Sorry to bother you..." "I just think..." "I could be wrong, but..."

Unnecessary apologies and qualifiers chip away at your credibility and presence. They tell people you're not confident in what you're saying, even if you are.

☑ **Reframe:** "I'll speak with clarity and let my words stand tall. No apology needed for taking up space."

3. Hiding Behind Perfectionism

"I'll speak up when I'm 100% sure."

Waiting to be perfect often leads to saying nothing at all. Leadership doesn't require flawlessness—it requires **courage and clarity**.

☑ **Reframe:** "Progress over perfection. My insight matters now."

4. Over-Explaining

"Let me give all the context so they really understand…"

Trying to justify your point too much can signal doubt. Trust that your words are enough.

☑ **Reframe:** "I communicate clearly and trust that my message lands."

5. Downplaying Your Success

"Oh, it was nothing…"

You've worked hard. Own your wins. Downplaying makes others doubt your credibility and dims your light.

☑ **Reframe:** "That was a big win, and I'm proud of what I accomplished."

Recognizing your presence pitfalls isn't about shame—it's about self-awareness and reclamation of your power. These habits don't make you weak or unworthy. They're simply learned behaviors, often shaped by environments that taught you to stay small, quiet, or agreeable. But the truth is, you were never meant to blend in—you were designed to stand in your brilliance.

Every time you choose to stop apologizing unnecessarily, speak with clarity, or take up space with confidence, you're rewriting the narrative. You're no longer living or leading from fear—you're leading with intention. And that shift? That's what changes how rooms receive you, how decisions include you, and how opportunities find you.

So, give yourself grace for where you've shrunk, then give yourself permission to rise. Your presence isn't just needed—it's *powerful.*

Mini Coaching Moment & Journal Prompt:

Take a moment and ask yourself the following questions and then write the responses in the space provided below or in your journal. Write freely. No filters. This is your time to reclaim the presence you've been holding back.

♟ Which of these presence pitfalls have I struggled with, and what will I do to rise above them starting now?

_____

_____

_____

_____

_____

♟ Where have I been shrinking, silencing, or second-guessing my presence? Why?

_____

_____

_____

_____

_____

♟ What would it look like to fully take up space in my next meeting, conversation, or opportunity?

_____

_____

_____

_____

_____

CHAPTER

PRACTICE PRESENCE AS A DAILY HABIT

As you reflected on your own presence, you may have uncovered moments where you've dimmed your light or questioned your worth. But awareness is just the beginning. True transformation happens when insights become action. Now it's time to take what you've discovered and bring it into your daily rhythm. Let's explore how to make presence a habit—one intentional choice, one powerful moment at a time.

Presence is practiced in the small moments, not just the big ones.

We often associate presence with performance—those high-stakes moments when all eyes are on us: leading a meeting, presenting to leadership, or commanding a room. But true presence isn't reserved for the spotlight. It's crafted in the quiet. Homed in the hallway. Built in the in-between.

Real presence is not a performance—it's a practice. It's the way you carry yourself when no one's watching, the tone you use when responding to a tense email, the posture you take when logging into a virtual call, and the mindset you choose each morning before your day begins.

Presence doesn't arrive fully formed. It's shaped in your habits, your choices, and your energy. The more intentional you are in small moments, the more powerful your presence becomes in the big ones.

So, how do you strengthen your presence when no one's watching? It starts with small, intentional choices. Below are simple but powerful habits you can practice daily to sharpen your awareness, elevate your energy, and show up with consistency and impact—no spotlight required.

Your Morning Mindset Routine

How you start your day directly influences how you show up. Are you rushing, reacting, and carrying yesterday's stress? Or are you grounding yourself in clarity, purpose, and peace?

Even 5–10 minutes in the morning can shift your energy. Whether through prayer, meditation, affirmations, journaling, or silence with your tea or coffee, start your day by aligning your mindset with your mission. Presence flows from a clear and centered mind.

How You Enter a Room (or Log onto a Call)

First impressions still matter—yes, even on video. The way you enter a room (physically or virtually) sets the tone. Are you dragging in apologetically? Entering distracted? Or are you arriving prepared?

When you enter with intention, you signal that you are someone to listen to. That doesn't mean you have to be dramatic or loud. It means you're grounded, aware, and owning your space, even in a simple introduction or greeting.

Non-Verbal Communication

Your body often speaks before your mouth does. Are your shoulders back? Is your eye contact strong but warm? Are you leaning in to listen or distracted by what you'll say next?

Active listening is a hidden superpower of presence. People can tell when you're fully present versus passively waiting to talk. Combine this with your tone—calm, confident, and clear—and you create an energy that commands attention without demanding it.

Consistency and Follow-Through

One of the most powerful presence builders? Being someone others can count on. Presence isn't just about how you show up—it's about whether people trust you to keep showing up. Do you meet deadlines? Follow through on your word? Return messages? Honor your boundaries?

When people know they can count on you, they view you as credible, professional, and anchored. That kind of quiet consistency builds trust faster than any flashy introduction ever could.

Your presence starts with your patterns.

Before we talk about building better habits, let's take a moment to check in with how you're showing up right now.

No pressure—just a quick, honest look at what's working and where there's room to grow.

Ready? The assessment is waiting for you on the next page.

Presence Self-Assessment: Score Your Daily Habits

Take a moment and complete the following **Presence Self-Assessment** to see how you're doing with your daily habits.

For each statement, score yourself from 1 to 5:
1. Never
2. Rarely
3. Sometimes
4. Often
5. Always

Add your total score at the end to reflect on where you're thriving and where there's room to grow.

Morning Mindset

- I start my day with intention (journaling, prayer, affirmations, etc.).
  Score (1–5): _____
- I align my mindset with my goals and values before starting work.
  Score (1–5): _____
- I avoid diving into emails or distractions first thing in the morning.
  Score (1–5): _____

Entering Spaces with Presence

- I enter meetings or spaces feeling mentally prepared and confident.
  Score (1–5): _____
- I take a moment to ground myself before joining a conversation.
  Score (1–5): _____

♟ I greet others with eye contact and presence, even virtually.
Score (1–5): _____

Nonverbal Communication

♟ My body language is confident, open, and grounded.
Score (1–5): _____

♟ I maintain appropriate eye contact and a calm tone of voice.
Score (1–5): _____

♟ I listen actively without interrupting or mentally checking out.
Score (1–5): _____

Consistency & Follow-Through

♟ I consistently follow through on my commitments.
Score (1–5): _____

♟ I communicate with professionalism and respect.
Score (1–5): _____

♟ I show up in every space I enter with the same excellence and energy.
Score (1–5): _____

Scoring Rubric

Add up your scores from all 12 questions. Use the guide below to reflect on your current presence habits.

+ **45–60**: Presence Powerhouse – You show up consistently with intention, alignment, and confidence. Keep sharpening and mentoring others!

+ **30–44**: Presence in Progress – You're building strong habits but may benefit from refining your consistency or energy in key moments.

+ **15–29**: Presence Pause – It's time for a mindset and habit reset. Start small by focusing on 1–2 areas you want to grow in.
+ **Below 15**: Presence Reboot – You're likely operating from autopilot or survival mode. This is your invitation to reconnect with your voice, value, and daily rhythm.

Reflection:

What did this assessment reveal about how I'm currently showing up? What's one habit I will focus on shifting this week?

_____

_____

_____

_____

_____

_____

NOTES

PART

03

VENTURE WITH INTENTION

MOVE WITH PURPOSE, NOT PRESSURE

CHAPTER

MAKING MOVES THAT MATTER

By now, you've done some powerful inner work. In the first part of this journey, we explored what leadership beyond titles and job descriptions really means. You've redefined your identity, uncovered your strengths, and challenged the limiting beliefs that have been holding you back. You've learned to master your mindset, own your presence, and show up in rooms with purpose and confidence. You've even begun shaping how others experience your Signature Move.

This next part of the Signature M.O.V.E.™ Framework is about what you do with all of that.

Venture with intention is your invitation to take action—not random, reactive action but bold, thoughtful, and strategic steps that align with your growth. This is where courage meets clarity. Where desire meets direction. And where your next move becomes less about being ready and more about being willing.

Too often, we wait for the "perfect" moment, the title, or someone else's permission to level up. But the truth is, opportunities are rarely handed over. You create them. You prepare for them. You declare them. Whether you're feeling the nudge to pivot careers, step into leadership, negotiate your value, or walk away from what's no longer in alignment, this is your moment.

To venture with intention is to move with purpose, not pressure. It's trusting the work you've done, listening to your inner wisdom, and making bold decisions that honor both your ambition and your alignment.

You didn't come this far to stay where you are. You came to grow.

Knowing When to Make Your Next Move

So, how do you know when it's time to go, grow, pivot, or leap forward? Do you just stumble into it, or do you move toward it with intention? That's what this part of the book is all about. We all reach a point in our professional journey when we start to sense a shift: a quiet restlessness, a tug toward something more, or the realization that we've outgrown the space we're in. The question isn't *if* these moments will come—it's whether we'll recognize them for what they are: invitations. And whether we'll respond with courage or settle into comfort.

The signs are usually there long before you're willing to acknowledge them. Maybe you no longer feel energized in your role. Maybe you're constantly questioning your value or wondering what would happen if you finally went for that promotion, new position, or next-level opportunity. Growth rarely announces itself with fanfare—it often whispers. Your job is to listen. When the same frustrations keep surfacing or you feel a pull toward something greater, that's not just dissatisfaction—it might be divine direction.

Sometimes, the boldest move isn't quitting your job—it's asking for what you deserve in the one you already have. We often wait for someone to notice our work, hand us a promotion, or validate our readiness. But waiting quietly rarely leads to growth. If you've been consistently adding value, building results, and leading without a title—that's your sign. It's time to speak up, ask for more, and stop apologizing for wanting what you've earned.

And then there are moments that ask for something even bigger: the leap. The career change. The relocation. The side hustle turning full-time business. Leaps are rarely convenient, but they are always catalytic. The difference between a leap and a reckless move is preparation. Have you done the work to clarify what you want? Can you name the skills and strengths you bring? Do you know what you're walking toward, not just what you're leaving? A leap with clarity becomes a launch.

Remember, the point isn't just movement—it's aligned movement. Every pivot, request, or leap should be rooted in purpose, not pressure. Ask yourself: Am I choosing this out of fear or alignment? Out of urgency or vision? When your answer is driven by growth, peace, and deep clarity—even if you're scared—that's how you know it's time to MOVE.

Coaching Case Study:
Helping Jennifer Own Her Next Move

Client: "Jennifer"
Role: Senior Director at a financial institution
Challenge: She felt stuck in a role that no longer stretched her. Despite external success, she wrestled with a quiet inner restlessness and the fear that voicing her desire for more might come across as ungrateful or overly ambitious.

Jennifer was a brilliant senior director at a large financial institution when she came to me for coaching. By all external measures, she was thriving—well-liked, consistently delivering results, and seen as reliable. But internally, she felt something she couldn't shake: restlessness. The spark that once made her feel energized in her role had faded. She wasn't unhappy, but she wasn't growing either. And she couldn't tell if she was just being impatient or if it was time to make a move.

In our first session, Jennifer said something I hear often from high-performing women: "I don't want to seem ungrateful, but I know I have more in me. I just don't know what to do with that feeling." Together, we unpacked her discomfort and reframed it, not as dissatisfaction but as a signal, a quiet nudge from within telling her that she had outgrown her current role. She wasn't being challenged. She was waiting to be noticed when it was time to start owning her growth out loud.

Through coaching, Jennifer was able to articulate her wins, clarify what she wanted next, and build the confidence to ask for it. She drafted a vision for a new hybrid role that better aligned with her strengths, outlined how she had already been leading without the next level role title, and prepared to present her case. When she finally sat down with her leader, she spoke from a place of clarity, data, and quiet authority. The result? A well-earned promotion, expanded responsibilities, and a new sense of agency over her career.

Jennifer's story is not unusual—it's powerful because it's familiar. You don't always need to leap to make progress. Sometimes, the move is in the ask. The clarity is in the pause. The shift is in the ownership.

Coaching Reflection Prompt:

- ♟ Have you been quietly waiting to be seen, chosen, or promoted?
- ♟ What would change if you stopped waiting and started owning your next move?

Career Growth Checklist: Is It Time to Move?

Is it time to pivot, ask for more, or move forward?

By now, you may be thinking about your own "Jennifer moment." Maybe there's a quiet nudge you've been ignoring. Or perhaps you're feeling stretched thin in a space you've outgrown. The question isn't whether you're capable—the real question is whether you're clear on what's next and willing to act on that clarity.

The checklist on the following pages is designed to help you assess where you are, where you're growing, and where it might be time to make your next move. This is not about quitting impulsively or chasing the next shiny thing. Nope! This is about strategic reflection that empowers you to lead your career instead of letting it happen to you.

As you go through the checklist, be honest. Don't just check the boxes you *wish* were true. (Yes, I'm calling you out.) You deserve a role, career, and leadership path that fits, not just the one you've been surviving.

Instructions:

For each statement, choose the option that best reflects your experience:

- ♟ Very True (1 point)
- ♟ Somewhat True (0.5 points)
- ♟ Not True at All (0 points)

Tally your total after each section. Then, reflect on your **overall score** to determine whether you're thriving, surviving, or ready for a shift.

Alignment Check – Am I in the right place for who I am now?

- ♟ I feel aligned with my current role, team, and organization's values.
  ☐ Very True (1 point)   ☐ Somewhat True (0.5 points)
  ☐ Not True at All (0 points)

- ♟ My work energizes and challenges me in a meaningful way.
  ☐ Very True (1 point)   ☐ Somewhat True (0.5 points)
  ☐ Not True at All (0 points)

- ♟ I can clearly see how my current role fits into my bigger career vision.
  ☐ Very True (1 point)   ☐ Somewhat True (0.5 points)
  ☐ Not True at All (0 points)

♖ I'm able to show up as my authentic self in my work environment.
☐ Very True (1 point)   ☐ Somewhat True (0.5 points)
☐ Not True at All (0 points)

♖ I feel respected and valued for my contributions.
☐ Very True (1 point)   ☐ Somewhat True (0.5 points)
☐ Not True at All (0 points)

→ Section Total: _____/5

Growth Check – Am I being stretched or stifled?

♖ I have regular opportunities to learn, lead, or take on meaningful challenges.
☐ Very True (1 point)   ☐ Somewhat True (0.5 points)
☐ Not True at All (0 points)

♖ I'm being compensated fairly and supported in my development.
☐ Very True (1 point)   ☐ Somewhat True (0.5 points)
☐ Not True at All (0 points)

♖ I've outgrown this role and am no longer being challenged.
☐ Very True (1 point)   ☐ Somewhat True (0.5 points)
☐ Not True at All (0 points)

♖ I find myself daydreaming about other possibilities or feeling stuck.
☐ Very True (1 point)   ☐ Somewhat True (0.5 points)
☐ Not True at All (0 points)

♖ I know I have more to offer, but I don't see the space to express it here.
☐ Very True (1 point)   ☐ Somewhat True (0.5 points)
☐ Not True at All (0 points)

→ Section Total: _____/5

Voice & Visibility Check – Am I being seen and heard?

♟ I feel confident sharing my ideas and insights in meetings and conversations.
☐ Very True (1 point)   ☐ Somewhat True (0.5 points)
☐ Not True at All (0 points)

♟ I have access to decision-makers and feel empowered to influence outcomes.
☐ Very True (1 point)   ☐ Somewhat True (0.5 points)
☐ Not True at All (0 points)

♟ I've been overlooked for roles or projects that align with my strengths.
☐ Very True (1 point)   ☐ Somewhat True (0.5 points)
☐ Not True at All (0 points)

♟ My voice, perspective, and potential are not being acknowledged consistently.
☐ Very True (1 point)   ☐ Somewhat True (0.5 points)
☐ Not True at All (0 points)

♟ I'm being invited into rooms but not into decisions.
☐ Very True (1 point)   ☐ Somewhat True (0.5 points)
☐ Not True at All (0 points)

→ Section Total: _____/5

Emotional & Mental Health Check – What's this costing me?

♟ I don't feel anxious, depleted, or overlooked at the end of most workdays.
☐ Very True (1 point)   ☐ Somewhat True (0.5 points)
☐ Not True at All (0 points)

♟ I'm not constantly questioning my worth or future here.
☐ Very True (1 point)   ☐ Somewhat True (0.5 points)
☐ Not True at All (0 points)

☖ I feel a sense of peace, possibility, and progress in my role.
☐ Very True (1 point)   ☐ Somewhat True (0.5 points)
☐ Not True at All (0 points)

☖ I've stayed in this space out of fear, comfort, or obligation, not alignment.
☐ Very True (1 point)   ☐ Somewhat True (0.5 points)
☐ Not True at All (0 points)

☖ The thought of moving on feels more freeing than frightening.
☐ Very True (1 point)   ☐ Somewhat True (0.5 points)
☐ Not True at All (0 points)

→ Section Total: _____/5

Scoring Your Checklist

Tally up your total score from each section. Use the guide below to interpret your results and determine what your next intentional career move might be.

☖ • Very True = 1 point

☖ • Somewhat True = 0.5 points

☖ • Not True at All = 0 points

Overall Score: _____/20

✦ ** 16–20**: You're thriving (aligned and growing). Stay and stretch where you are!

✦ **10–15.5**: You're surviving (in the gray zone). Time to get curious, advocate, or explore what's next.

✦ **Below 10**: Time for a shift. It could be time to start planning your next move.

Reflection:

What is your career trying to tell you right now, and what would it mean to truly listen?

_____

_____

_____

_____

_____

When was the last time you felt fully stretched in your role in a way that energized you rather than drained you? What conditions made that growth possible, and how can you create more of them?

_____

_____

_____

_____

_____

What is the "hidden cost" you're currently paying to stay in your role (stress, self-doubt, or exhaustion) and what boundaries or supports could help reduce that cost?

_____

_____

_____

_____

_____

NOTES

CHAPTER

KNOWING YOUR WORTH (AND ASKING FOR IT)

> *You can't elevate your life*
> *if you keep negotiating away your value.*

There comes a point in every growth journey when the next move isn't just about where you're going—it's about how you see yourself on the way there. The last chapter helped you discern when it's time to shift, stretch, or leap. But what comes next is just as crucial: having the courage to name your value, ask for what you need, and stand in your worth without flinching. Advocating for your value is one of the boldest, most intentional moves you can make.

Let's be real—many of us have spent years over-delivering and under-asking. We've played the "grateful to be here" game while silently carrying workloads, leading behind the scenes, or staying stuck in roles we outgrew two promotions prior. And somewhere along the way, we started confusing humility with silence. We started believing that asking for more would make us "too much."

But not anymore.

This chapter is your sign to disrupt that pattern, not with arrogance but with alignment. Not with entitlement—but with evidence (or receipts!). You're not asking for favors. You're advocating from a place of clarity, preparation, and power. And the moment you stop waiting to be seen and start speaking from your seat of value, you shift the entire room.

So, let's get to it. Let's talk about the mindset, strategy, and courage it takes to advocate for yourself unapologetically and negotiate what you're worth because shrinking isn't noble, and silence won't take you where you're called to go.

Self-Advocacy

If you don't advocate for yourself, who will?

Self-advocacy is more than a skill, it's a mindset. It's the belief that your voice matters, your needs are valid, and your growth is worth speaking up for. For too long, many women (including myself) have internalized the idea that to be likable is to be low-maintenance. That to be a "team player" means to stay quiet, say "yes" to everything, and hope someone notices the effort.

But let's be clear: You can be kind and still set boundaries. You can be humble and still ask for more. You can be collaborative and still be seen.

You don't need to be loud, forceful, or aggressive to advocate for yourself. You just need to **be clear**. You need to know what you want, what you need, and why it matters to your growth and the organization. And then, you need to **say it with calm confidence**, even when your voice shakes.

Self-Advocacy in Action Is:

- ♟ Asking for a stretch role without waiting to be invited
- ♟ Speaking up in meetings where you've stayed silent too long
- ♟ Setting boundaries around your time, energy, and workload
- ♟ Requesting feedback or support instead of trying to "figure it out alone"
- ♟ Naming the impact you've made instead of downplaying it

Self-advocacy doesn't mean you're demanding or difficult. It means you value your voice enough to use it and trust your worth enough to protect it.

Why It's Hard (But Worth It)

Let's be real. Advocating for yourself isn't always easy.

Many of us were raised to play it safe, to keep the peace, to be grateful just to have a seat at the table. That conditioning runs deep, and it can make speaking up feel uncomfortable, even risky. You might worry that you'll come across as pushy, ungrateful, or worse... that people won't take you seriously.

But here's the truth: staying quiet comes with its own cost. When you don't advocate for yourself, you start to carry unspoken frustration. You shrink your presence without even realizing it. And over time, people assume your silence means you're fine where you are. They stop looking your way, not because you lack the talent, but because you haven't given them a reason to expect your voice in the room.

The good news? Every time you choose to speak up, you make it easier the next time. You build that muscle. And slowly, you stop being the one who waits for opportunities to come your way. You become the one who steps into alignment with who you are and what you deserve.

Self-Advocacy Is a Leadership Skill.

The more you advocate for yourself, the more you build your capacity to advocate for others. Your courage creates ripple effects. You become the woman who opens doors, challenges norms, and shows other women what's possible.

- ♟ This is leadership in motion.
- ♟ This is your Signature Move in action.
- ♟ This is what it means to venture with intention.

How to Negotiate with Confidence and Clarity

You've just reclaimed one of the most powerful tools you have: your voice. But now that you've found your voice, what do you do with it? You use it to ask. You use it to initiate conversations that open doors, close deals, elevate your career, and align your role with your value. That's where negotiation comes in, not as a battle but as a bold, clear declaration of who you are, what you bring, and what you're ready to walk into next.

Negotiation is not about demanding, it's about declaring your value with clarity and calm authority. It's one of the most empowering skills a woman can master, and yet, for so many, it still feels uncomfortable, intimidating, or even taboo. Why? Because we've been conditioned to believe that asking for more makes us "ungrateful" or "difficult." We believe if we ask, we might talk ourselves out of a good opportunity.

Let's be clear: Negotiation is not a confrontation. It's a conversation rooted in facts and framed with confidence. Whether you're negotiating a salary, title, workload, stretch opportunity, or business deal, preparation is everything! That means knowing your worth in the market, understanding your contributions to the organization, and having the language to make your ask with strength and grace.

Your clarity fuels your confidence. The more specific you are about what you want and why you deserve it, the easier it is to silence the inner critic that says, "Just be thankful for what you have." Confidence doesn't mean you won't feel nervous; it means you don't let fear do the talking. When you negotiate from a place of self-awareness and strategic positioning, you shift the narrative from "I hope I get it" to "Here's what I bring, and here's what I'm asking."

Stepping into our courage zone and flexing our negotiation skills means saying out loud what we've often hoped others would just see for themselves. And if you've ever walked away from a conversation thinking, "I should've asked for more" or "Maybe I could have pushed just a little further," you're not the only one.

I know that feeling well. Like so many women, I've stayed in roles, held onto titles, or accepted compensation that didn't reflect my true value. Not because I wasn't ready for more, but because I'd been conditioned to wait my turn, to keep the peace, or to prove myself just a little longer.

But here's the shift: it's time to flip that script and move forward with intention. That's exactly what Danielle chose to do.

Coaching Case Study:
Helping Danielle Find Her Voice at the Table

Client: "Danielle"
Role: Senior Analyst at a large tech company
Challenge: She struggled with balancing her desire to be recognized for her contributions with her fear of being seen as disruptive.

Danielle came to one of our coaching sessions feeling undervalued and overlooked. She'd been in her role as a senior analyst for three years, had taken on leadership responsibilities well beyond her title, and was mentoring junior staff while still managing a full workload. "I just don't want to rock the boat," she said, "but I also can't keep pretending that I'm okay with being passed over."

We began unpacking her discomfort, not to make her wrong for feeling it but to uncover the truth beneath it. Danielle wasn't ungrateful; she was ready. Ready to ask for a title that reflected her contributions. Ready to speak up in leadership meetings instead of waiting to be invited. And ready to stop shrinking in rooms she had clearly earned a seat in.

Together, we prepared her negotiation plan: a clear ask, proof of performance, and language that positioned her not just as someone who wanted more but as someone who had *already been operating* at the next level. I encouraged her to reframe the conversation from confrontation to collaboration. The result? Danielle made two attempts and was successful on her second try. She didn't just walk away with a new title and raise—she walked away with ownership of her voice. Her growth didn't start when she got the promotion—it started when she chose to advocate for herself.

Danielle's story is a powerful reminder that staying silent doesn't protect your peace—it often postpones your progress. The ability to negotiate for what you deserve and advocate for what you need isn't a luxury—it's a leadership skill.

Let's walk through a few practical tips to help you get prepared for your next important conversation.

Tips to Negotiate & Self-Advocate

Whether you're preparing for a compensation conversation, role transition, or boundary-setting moment, these coaching insights will help prepare you.

Shift Your Mindset: You're Not Asking for a Favor

Before you walk into the room, you need to walk into a different mindset. This isn't about hoping they say "yes." This is about positioning the value you bring and making a confident, informed ask. When you enter prepared, with evidence and clarity, the conversation shifts. You're not begging—you're building a case.

Ask yourself:

- ♟ What results have I delivered that have impacted the team or business?
- ♟ What responsibilities or leadership have I taken on that go beyond my current role?
- ♟ How have I grown, and how can I grow more?
- ♟ What do I really want, and why do I hesitate to ask for it?

Own your contribution. Lead with outcomes. Present your case as someone who has *already been operating* at the next level.

Be Prepared with Data and Direction

The most powerful negotiators don't just know their value—they can articulate it. Frame it around impact, not emotion. Bring metrics, performance reviews, client feedback, completed projects, team wins, and personal milestones. You are not just asking to be recognized—you are making it easier for the other party to say "yes" by doing the thinking for them.

- ● Say: "Here's the impact I've made and how I'd like to grow in alignment with that impact."

But don't stop at what you've done. Come prepared to share what you want.

- ♟ Is it a title change? A compensation adjustment? A new opportunity?
- ♟ What's your desired outcome, and what alternatives are acceptable?
- ♟ What value will your ask create for the organization?

Remember: Clarity eliminates confusion and confident, prepared people are taken seriously.

Script Your Key Points & Practice Out Loud

You don't have to script every word, but practicing how you'll start the conversation matters. Confidence grows through repetition. Practice with a friend, coach, or mirror. You don't want your first time saying it to be in the meeting.

The first 30 seconds often set the tone. Practice phrases like:

- ♟ "I've been reflecting on the contributions I've made and the direction I'm headed, and I'd love to have a conversation about how my role can evolve."
- ♟ "I'm really proud of the impact I've had over the last year. I'd like to explore how that could be reflected in my next step."

When you speak with calm certainty, you give the conversation structure and lead it.

Let Go of "I'm Sorry" Language

No more shrinking sentences like:

- ☒ "I hope this isn't asking for too much..."
- ☒ "I know you're busy but..."
- ☒ "I just wanted to ask if maybe..."

Replace them with empowered, language like:

- ☑ "I'd like to propose..."
- ☑ "Here's what I'm requesting based on the results I've delivered..."
- ☑ "This conversation is important, and I'm looking forward to your thoughts."

You can be humble and direct. Negotiating well doesn't compromise your character—it strengthens your leadership.

Exercise:
Your Negotiation Plan – What's Your Ask?

You've done the mindset work. You've explored your growth, named your value, and committed to showing up differently. Now, it's time to get clear on your next bold step and create a plan to ask for it with strategy and confidence.

Use this negotiation planning tool as a personal blueprint to organize your thoughts and prepare for your next growth conversation—a raise, promotion, new title, stretch role, or boundary shift.

STEP 1:

DEFINE WHAT YOU'RE ASKING FOR

Get crystal clear on your specific ask. Don't water it down or over-explain—just state it boldly.

Prompt:

What are you asking for? (Title, raise, stretch assignment, support, resources, etc.)

Example: I am asking for a promotion to senior manager with a 15% salary increase to reflect the expanded scope and leadership I've already been delivering.

✏ **My ask is:**

_____

_____

_____

_____

STEP 2:

GATHER THE EVIDENCE

List 3–5 specific results, wins, or contributions that demonstrate your value. These are your **receipts**—the proof points that justify your ask.

Prompt:

What have you delivered that shows you're ready for this next level?

📎 **Evidence:**

1. _____
2. _____
3. _____
4. _____
5. _____

STEP 3:

CLARIFY THE WHY

Your negotiation is stronger when it's rooted in purpose, not pressure. Why is this ask aligned with your growth?

Prompt:

How does this next step align with your long-term vision and leadership goals?

✏️ **My "why" behind the ask is:**

_____
_____
_____

STEP 4:

PREPARE FOR PUSHBACK

Anticipate hesitation or questions and craft a confident response in advance. This isn't about being defensive—it's about being ready.

Prompt:

What objections might they raise? What concerns could they have?

✎ **Potential pushback:**

_____

_____

🗣 **My response:**

_____

_____

STEP 5:

PRACTICE YOUR POWER PHRASES

Write out 1–2 bold phrases that you'll use in the conversation. Rehearsing your tone and words builds confidence.

Examples:

- ♟ "I'm excited about the results I've delivered and the opportunity to grow further in alignment with the organization's goals."

- ♟ "I believe this step reflects the leadership I'm already demonstrating and positions me to deliver even greater impact."

✎ **My power phrases:**

1. _____
2. _____
3. _____

STEP 6:

DECIDE WHAT HAPPENS NEXT

Negotiation isn't one-and-done—it's a dialogue. What's your plan if you hear "yes," "no," or "not yet"?

Prompt:

What will be your next step in each of these scenarios?

✔ If the answer is "Yes":

_____

_____

✔ If the answer is "No":

_____

_____

✔ If the answer is "Not Yet":

_____

_____

Reflection Prompt:

What did you learn about yourself by preparing for this conversation?

_____

_____

_____

_____

_____

_____

What part of making the ask felt most challenging for you, and why do you think that was?

_____

_____

_____

_____

_____

How might you apply what you practiced today to a real negotiation you're preparing for in your career or personal life?

_____

_____

_____

_____

_____

PART

04

EXPAND YOUR IMPACT

SHIFTING FROM SUCCESS TO
SIGNIFICANCE

CHAPTER

BUILDING A BRILLIANT NETWORK

66 ─────────

Your greatest impact won't come from what you achieve alone—
it will come from what you ignite in others.

DR. DEYONNE PARKER

───────── 99

By now, you've done some deep work. You've mastered your mindset, owned your presence, ventured with intention, and asked for what you deserve. But your journey doesn't end at the door you just opened. True leadership, the kind that transforms, isn't about how far you climb. It's about how many people you bring with you.

This chapter is where your Signature Move grows roots and becomes *more than a personal win.* It becomes a ripple. A movement. A legacy. Because real impact doesn't happen in isolation, it happens in community, collaboration, and meaningful connections.

Expanding your impact means shifting from success to significance. It means being intentional about how you build relationships, show up in rooms that matter, and *make room* for others. Whether you're finding your next bold move or mentoring the next woman who reminds you of yourself, you are building something that lasts.

Let's talk about mentorship, sponsorship, networking with soul (not just strategy), and creating a legacy that outlives your LinkedIn profile. Because your Signature Move isn't just yours to keep—it's yours to multiply.

66 ⸻⸻⸻⸻⸻⸻⸻

Your success is the seed of someone else's breakthrough.

ZIG ZIGLAR
⸻⸻⸻⸻⸻⸻ **99**

Finding Mentors, Sponsors & Support Circles

Every bold move, every breakthrough, every door that swings open often traces back to a single connection. A mentor who gave you wisdom. A sponsor who spoke your name in a room full of opportunity. A sister from your circle who reminded you who you were when you started to forget. These relationships aren't just helpful—they're essential for sustainable growth and lasting impact.

Up until now, you might have tried to do it all on your own—shouldering the pressure, navigating unfamiliar spaces, and hoping someone noticed. But here's the truth: Growth accelerates when you're supported, seen, and surrounded. You don't need to wait until you have it all together to seek guidance or connection. You just need to be willing to *receive*.

What's the Difference?

It's important to understand the differences between the various roles of the people that support you. Each role serves a specific purpose, and you'll likely need all four at different points on your journey.

- ♟ **Mentors** pour into you. They share wisdom, guidance, and lessons learned from experience. They help you grow.
- ♟ **Coaches** challenge your thinking. They ask you thought-provoking questions to help you dig deep to find and own your solutions. They help you see things you didn't see before and try things you wouldn't normally try.
- ♟ **Sponsors** advocate for you. They use their influence to open doors, position your name, and recommend you when you're not in the room.
- ♟ **Support circles** walk with you. These are your iron-sharpeners—the people who keep you grounded, uplifted, and accountable.

Just like the Queen on a chessboard doesn't win the game alone, neither do you. Every piece has a role to play—just as mentors, coaches, sponsors, and support circles each serve a distinct purpose on your journey. The Queen moves with power because she's aware of the team around her. In the same way, your strength is amplified by those who guide you, challenge you, advocate for you, and stand beside you. Build your board with intention—because every winning move is supported by a strategy, and every bold step is backed by a circle.

My Personal Board of Executive Advisors

When I reflect on my own growth, I can trace it back to the voices that spoke into me. I call them my personal board of executive advisors. There were my mentors who helped me own my gifts when I doubted myself. My sponsors who believed in my value and made one bold introduction that led to a life-changing opportunity. And the circle of women and men who prayed with, challenged, and reminded me that I didn't have to carry everything all alone.

My growth didn't rest on strategy alone—I grew because I let others lift, pour into, and speak truth over me.

And now, as I have the distinct privilege to coach and mentor others, advocate for the women around me, and build spaces where brilliance is multiplied, I realize this is how we expand our impact. It's not by building empires alone but by building each other.

Your personal board doesn't have to be large. It just needs to be aligned, intentional, and reciprocal. Build it with care. Nurture it with consistency. Make sure you are giving back to them as much as they are giving to you. It is truly a gift to have people to care enough about you to support you through your life's journey.

Reflection Prompt:

- ♖ Who is pouring into you?
- ♖ Who is advocating for you?
- ♖ And who are you surrounding yourself with that helps you stay grounded and growing?

The following activity will help you identify the voices that support you.

Exercise: Mapping Your Support Circle

The people in your circle help shape your perspective, pace, and possibilities.

This exercise is designed to help you visualize the relationships that currently support your growth and identify where you may need to build or deepen connections with mentors, sponsors, or support circles.

You're not meant to walk this journey alone, and you shouldn't have to guess who's in your corner.

STEP 1:

WHO SUPPORTS YOU?

Write the names of people in your life who currently serve in the following roles or whom you'd like to invite into these roles. (It's okay if some areas are blank. This is about clarity, not perfection.)

ROLE	NAME	HOW DO THEY SUPPORT ME?
Mentor		
Sponsor		
Coach		
Support Circle		

STEP 2:

WHERE ARE THE GAPS?

Ask yourself:

- Do I have someone I can go to for honest advice?
- Is anyone currently advocating for me when I'm not in the room?
- Am I constantly surrounded by people who want to see me win?
- Where am I over-relying on one person or trying to do too much alone?

STEP 3:

What Do You Need Next?

Choose one action step you'll take this month to build or strengthen a relationship in your circle.

⚓ *My next intentional connection is:* _____

📅 *By this date:* _____

✉ *How I will reach out or show up:*

_____

_____

Networking with Intention

I know...I know. You are cringing just reading the word networking. You're not alone. I used to feel this way. Let's reframe the word. For many people—especially those who are introverted, thoughtful, or simply done with surface-level small talk—networking can feel transactional, awkward, or draining. But here's the truth: Networking isn't about collecting business cards—it's about cultivating relationships.

If you've ever felt like networking just isn't for you, this is your time to redefine what it can look like. Because when done with purpose and presence, networking becomes one of the most powerful ways to expand your impact, open new doors, and align with people who can grow alongside you.

Some of the most transformational relationships I've formed didn't come from me "selling myself." They came from me being fully present, genuinely curious, and willing to speak purposefully when it mattered most.

Reframe It: Networking Is About Alignment, Not Access

Instead of asking, "Who should I meet?" ask, "Who aligns with where I'm going?"

Instead of focusing on quantity, focus on quality connections—people who share your values, stretch your thinking, or support your vision. The most impactful relationships often begin with one authentic conversation, not a dozen shallow ones.

Before you head to any networking event, plan your approach so it doesn't feel so daunting. Know who might be in the room and what the format of the event will be. This helps you to focus on those quality connections and minimizes the angst you might feel in the moment.

Tips for Networking with Presence (Not Pressure)

1. Lead with Curiosity, Not Credentials

Instead of launching into your elevator pitch, ask thoughtful questions.

- ❏ "What project are you most excited about right now?"
- ❏ "What inspired you to do this work?"

2. Be Seen Where You Want to Grow

Attend events, workshops, or spaces where the conversations stretch you, not just where you're comfortable. Put yourself in rooms that reflect your next level.

3. Follow Up like a Leader

Networking isn't just about the introduction—it's about the follow-through. Send a message. Share a resource. Offer support. Add value, not noise.

4. Honor Your Energy

> If you're introverted, shy or new to networking, build in recovery time. Set a realistic goal like making 1–2 meaningful connections at an event instead of working the entire room.

Now that you've laid the groundwork for meaningful connections, it's time to pause, reflect, and recalibrate. Because every Queen eventually faces the question: *What's my next move?* Let's explore how to answer that in the next chapter.

12

WHAT'S YOUR NEXT MOVE?

The right relationships can open doors, stretch your perspective, and remind you of what's possible. But no matter how powerful your network becomes; it won't move you forward without clarity. Your next step requires more than connections—it requires **vision** that helps you say "yes" to the right opportunities and "no" to distractions. This chapter will help you pause, zoom out, and align with your *next bold move*—the one that reflects who you are, what you're called to build, and the impact you're ready to make.

Ready? Let's do it!

Write the Vision

This is your space to dream boldly, think clearly, and align deeply. Whether you're at a crossroads, entering a new season, or feeling the nudge to expand your reach—this visioning activity will help you name what's next with intention and purpose.

Find a quiet moment. Breathe deeply. Grab your journal or a blank page and lean in.

PART 1:

STEP INTO THE FUTURE

Close your eyes and imagine yourself three years from now.

- ♖ Where are you?
- ♖ What kind of work are you doing?
- ♖ How do you feel in your day-to-day life?
- ♖ What rooms are you walking into?
- ♖ What kind of presence do you carry?
- ♖ Who are you leading, influencing, or serving?
- ♖ What are people saying about your impact?

✎ **Describe this future version of yourself in detail.**

_____

_____

_____

PART 2:

IDENTIFY YOUR NEXT BOLD MOVE

Now bring it closer to the present. Ask yourself:

- ♖ What is one bold decision or step I need to take to move toward that vision?
- ♖ What have I been hesitating about that's actually aligned with where I'm going?
- ♖ What would I do if I wasn't afraid?

✎ **My next bold move is:**

_____

_____

_____

PART 3:

Name the Mindset You'll Need

Big vision requires big belief. What mindset shift must you adopt to step into that version of yourself?

- ♟ What belief do you need to strengthen?
- ♟ What fear or self-doubt do you need to release?

✏ **The mindset I choose to embody moving forward is:**

_____

_____

_____

PART 4:

Anchor the Vision

Complete the statement below as your personal declaration:

I am ready to make my next bold move because I know that_____

_____

Congratulations! Writing the vision is a bold first move—it gets your dreams out of your head and onto the page. But clarity doesn't end with a few sentences in a journal. To truly build a life and career that reflects your purpose, you have to stretch your thinking beyond the present moment. The next step is to lift your eyes from the page and ask yourself: *Where is all of this leading?* It's time to zoom out and define the long-term vision that will guide your decisions, align your goals, and anchor your next chapter.

Turning Vision Into Direction

Now that you've stretched your imagination and allowed yourself to dream boldly, it's time to think about how that vision can guide your next moves. A dream without direction can feel exciting in the moment, but a true vision serves as a steady anchor when distractions, doubts, or shiny opportunities show up.

Having a long-term vision doesn't mean you need every step mapped out. It's not about knowing the exact job title you'll hold or the precise timeline for getting there. It's about having a clear sense of who you want to become and the kind of impact you want your work (and your life) to make.

I know what it feels like to keep chasing the next project, promotion, or partnership, only to end up feeling restless and disconnected. I was moving quickly but without an anchor. What shifted everything for me was asking a simple but powerful question:

What's the story I want my life to tell?

That question reframed everything. It helped me stop building a career on autopilot and start making choices that aligned with the bigger picture of who I was becoming. Because clarity doesn't come from checking more boxes, it comes from having a vision that keeps pulling you forward.

Journaling Prompt:

Take a few minutes to capture what stood out to you during the visioning activity. Ask yourself:

♟ What pieces of my vision feel most alive or energizing right now?

_____

_____

_____

♟ How does this vision connect to the kind of impact I want my life to have?

_____

_____

_____

♟ If I could write one sentence that sums up the story I want my life to tell, what would it be?

_____

_____

_____

Let this reflection guide how you move from dreaming to designing your next steps.

66
"You can build a beautiful career and still feel empty if it isn't anchored in vision."

DR. DEYONNE PARKER
99

From Vision to Action: Building a Roadmap

Think of your roadmap as the bridge between your bold vision and your everyday choices. It breaks down what feels big and far off into smaller, doable moves that build momentum over time.

Here are three steps to help you design yours:

1. **Define Milestones:** Look at your long-term vision and identify a few key markers along the way. These aren't just job titles or promotions, they can also be experiences, skills, or impact moments you want to create. Milestones keep you motivated and give you something concrete to aim toward.

2. **Identify Growth Moves:** For each milestone, ask yourself: What skills, partners, or opportunities will help me get there? This might mean strengthening your leadership presence, building a new technical skill, expanding your network, or asking for stretch assignments.

3. **Set Near-Term Actions:** Now zoom into the next 90 days. What's one action you can take this quarter that moves you closer to your vision? Maybe it's having a career conversation with your manager, enrolling in a course, or carving out time for reflection and skill-building. Small, consistent steps are what make a vision real.

Remember: a roadmap isn't about predicting the future, it's about preparing for it. The most important part is to keep checking in with yourself. Is this path still aligned with who I'm becoming? If yes, keep moving. If not, adjust and realign.

Once you've envisioned your next move and positioned yourself with purpose, the game doesn't end, it evolves. Like a seasoned queen on the board, your power multiplies when you move with strategy and support others in doing the same. True mastery isn't just about protecting your position; it's about empowering other women to claim their space, make bold moves, and shift the game.

In the next chapter, we'll explore what it means to pay it forward and help other women shine because when one woman rises with intention, she creates a pathway for others to rise with her.

"Without vision, achievement becomes a performance. With vision, it becomes a calling."

DR. DEYONNE PARKER

13

PAYING IT FORWARD – HELPING OTHER WOMEN SHINE

You didn't come this far just to stand at the top alone. You came to create space. To build bridges. To be the woman who reaches back and says, "Come with me."

This final chapter is not about your next move—it's about your next multiplication. Success becomes even more meaningful when it's shared. You've grown, you've clarified your Signature Move, and you've activated your presence. Now, the question is: How will you use it to elevate others?

Mentorship: Walking with, Not Talking At

Mentoring is a privilege I don't take lightly. One of the greatest joys of my journey is to pour forward the lessons, wins, and even the hard-earned wisdom from my failures so another woman can rise with greater clarity and confidence. I've had the honor of mentoring countless women over the years, and nothing compares to witnessing them soar into the fullness of who they're called to be.

Mentorship isn't about having all the answers—it's about showing up with authenticity and intention. You don't have to have it all figured out to walk with another woman. You just have to be a little ahead, a little wiser, or simply willing to listen and pour back.

Mentorship is where your lessons become someone else's lifeline. It's how you take what you've lived through, struggled with, and learned to make it easier for someone else to rise.

Ask yourself:

- ♟ Who needs what I once needed?
- ♟ What do I wish someone had told me sooner?

You don't need a formal title to be a mentor—just an open heart and intentional spirit.

Advocacy: Say Her Name in Rooms She's Not In

Remember when we talked about speaking up for yourself? Now, we're flipping the script and focusing on how you can speak up for someone else. Advocacy is more than mentorship. It's not just offering encouragement behind the scenes—it's putting someone's name on the table when opportunities are on the line. It's using your access, influence, and seat to make sure another woman gets seen, heard, and positioned. Sponsors and advocates don't just cheer from the sidelines—they call her name at the table. They say, "I know someone who's ready," or "You should take a look at her."

You probably remember what it felt like to be overlooked, underestimated, or not considered because no one was there to speak for you. That experience stays with you, and it's exactly why your voice, now more than ever, is a powerful tool to create equity and opportunity for others. Change the narrative for someone else. Share the stage. Pass the mic. **Bring her Signature Move in the room.**

Here's the truth: *The room you're in is not just for you*. And you didn't get there alone.

True advocacy isn't competition—it's legacy.

Advocacy in Action Is:

- Recommending someone for a high-visibility project
- Speaking someone's name in decision-making conversations
- Writing a bold LinkedIn endorsement or reference
- Introducing a woman to someone in your network who can help her grow
- Repeating and affirming someone's idea when it gets talked over or dismissed in a meeting
- Declining an opportunity and recommending another brilliant woman instead

You don't need a title to be an advocate. You need intention—a willingness to use your platform, even if it feels small, to create space for another woman to rise.

Some of the most meaningful feedback I've ever received wasn't about my success—it was from women who said, "You spoke my name when I wasn't in the room." That is legacy. That is leadership. That is the ripple effect of living your Signature Move out loud.

Reflection:

- Whose name(s) are you carrying into rooms right now?
- Where can your voice create visibility, access, or affirmation for someone else?

Making Room at the Table

Real leadership is not about being the only one at the table—it's about ensuring you're not the last.

Throughout my journey, I've been given seats at incredible tables. And I've also sat at tables where I was talked over, doubted, or tolerated. I made a decision early on: When I finally have a seat, I will pull up more chairs. I will not be the only. That's the kind of leader I strive to be—one who multiplies, not just achieves.

If you've ever been the "first" or the "only" in a room, you know how heavy that title can feel. It comes with pride but also pressure. The truth is, breaking barriers is only half the story. The other half is making sure those barriers stay down for the women coming behind you.

Making room at the table means resisting the urge to protect your position and choosing instead to multiply opportunity. It's the difference between seeing your success as a finish line or a foundation for someone else's breakthrough.

But here's the part that often gets overlooked: Making room doesn't always look like grand gestures or public applause. Sometimes, it looks like:

- Inviting someone younger or less experienced to sit in on a strategy meeting
- Asking the question, "Whose voice hasn't been heard yet?" in a group
- Encouraging a woman to speak up and backing her when she does
- Modeling what inclusive, courageous leadership actually looks like

But what if there's no table? Then you build one. You bring your own chair—just like Shirley Chisholm said. And if a table isn't the answer, you form a circle. Because legacy isn't just about what you accomplish—it's about who you bring along and how you make space for others to rise with you.

Your story, your strength, and your courage were never meant to stay contained. They're meant to ripple out—to multiply, to open doors for others, to spark change. You are more than a leader. You are a multiplier, a bridge, a catalyst.

Reflection:

- Who is currently sitting at your table? Who's missing?
- And how can you create more space, visibility, and opportunity?

NOTES

CONCLUSION

MAKE YOUR SIGNATURE MOVE

You made it! You've journeyed through the **Signature M.O.V.E.™ Framework**, doing the inner work, naming bold decisions, challenging old beliefs, and learning to advocate for your worth without apology. You've mapped your impact, reimagined your vision, and committed to creating space for others to rise.

Now comes the part only you can do: **Make your Signature Move.**

Not someday. Not when everything feels perfect. **Today.**

Like the Queen on the chessboard—the most powerful and strategic piece in the game—you were designed to move boldly, lead with intention, and shift the momentum with every step. You don't need permission. You are the permission. You are resilience. You are range. You are radiant authority in motion.

Your Signature Move isn't just an idea. It's the way you show up in the world with clarity, confidence, and courage. It's how you influence, inspire, and ignite change. It's how you remind yourself and others that readiness is overrated, but movement changes everything.

So don't wait. The board is set. The moment is now.

Your move, Queen. ♛

Dr. DeYonne
PARKER

A Bold Affirmation

Read this out loud. Let it settle in your spirit. Come back to it whenever you forget who you are.

> I am a woman of clarity, confidence, and courage.
> I know my worth, I own my voice, and I walk in purpose.
> I am not defined by titles or timelines—I am led by vision.
> I do not shrink, I do not settle, and I will not wait to be chosen.
> I was built for this moment.
> And I will make my Signature Move boldly, fearlessly, and without apology.

Your Signature Move Commitment

Before you close this book, commit to taking one bold step toward your next move. Choose something simple, meaningful, and immediate. Because this is your moment—and it's time to MOVE.

Examples:

- ♟ Define or refine your Signature Move and say it aloud.
- ♟ Reach out to a potential mentor or sponsor and introduce yourself.
- ♟ Share your Signature Move publicly on social media or with a trusted circle.
- ♟ Say "no" to something that no longer aligns with your vision.
- ♟ Say "yes" to something that scares you in the best way.
- ♟ Schedule a data-driven career conversation with your leader.

✍ I commit to taking this action within the next 7 days: _____

_____

📅 Date I will do it by: _____

✒ Signed: _____

ACKNOWLEDGMENTS & CREDITS

No bold move is ever made alone—this book is no exception.

I am deeply grateful to every woman, mentor, coach, colleague, and courageous soul whose story, strength, or struggle helped shape this message. Whether you've sat across from me in a coaching session, invited me along on your leadership journey, allowed me the privilege to lead you, or shared a sacred moment of truth with me, you are part of the legacy this book aims to build.

Frameworks & Original Concepts

The **Signature M.O.V.E.™ Framework**—Master Your Mindset, Own Your Presence & Personal Brand, Venture with Intention, Expand Your Impact—is an original model developed to help women (and others who find this work beneficial) unlock their Signature Move.

All exercises, assessments, reflections, and journal prompts within this book were uniquely designed for this body of work unless otherwise noted.

Tools & Inspiration

Some activities and concepts were informed by widely respected coaching and personal development practices, including:

- ♟ **CliftonStrengths®** by Gallup – Strengths-based language and principles were used in shaping the Discovering Your Signature Move.

- ♟ **The Energy Project by Tony Schwartz** – Inspired the creation of the Energy Check and Boundary Builder exercises, which were adapted and written originally for this book.

Quotes & References

The following quotes appear in this book and are used with appreciation:

- ♟ *"You can't elevate your life if you keep negotiating away your value."* — *author unknown*

- ♟ *"Your greatest impact won't come from what you achieve alone—it will come from what you ignite in others."* — *Dr. DeYonne Parker*

- ♟ *"Doubt and fear kill more dreams than failure ever will."* — *Widely circulated quote, author unknown*

- ♟ *"You can build a beautiful career and still feel empty if it isn't anchored in vision."* - *Dr. DeYonne Parker*

- ♟ *"Without vision, achievement becomes a performance. With vision, it becomes a calling."* - *Dr. DeYonne Parker*

- ♟ *"Your success is the seed of someone else's breakthrough."* - *Zig Ziglar*

Any mention of public figures such as **Sarah Jakes Roberts** is used to illustrate mindset examples and is paraphrased based on publicly available information.

ABOUT THE AUTHOR

Dr. DeYonne "Dee" Parker is not just a leadership coach—she's a movement. A globally recognized speaker, author, and transformation strategist, Dr. Dee is affectionately known as *The Courage Catalyst*, a title earned from the countless women and leaders she's helped rise from hesitation to bold, unapologetic impact.

With over two decades of learning and leadership development experience in the corporate world and a lifelong commitment to women's empowerment, Dr. Dee has coached and developed mid to senior-level leaders, mentored emerging leaders, and inspired women across continents to lead with clarity, confidence, and courage.

As the creator of the **Your Signature Move™** brand and originator of the **Signature M.O.V.E.™ Framework**, she equips women with the mindset, strategy, and soul work needed to own their influence and walk boldly in purpose. Her teachings blend deep faith with practical leadership development, helping women of all backgrounds lead from a place of authenticity and intention.

She is the author of multiple empowering works, including *From Comfort to Courage*, *If Her Purse Could Talk*, and *Girl, Get Your S.W.A.G. Back!*—and the voice behind the popular podcast of the same name, inspiring women to reclaim their strength and shine.

Dr. Dee is also the co-founder of Gem Makers, LLC, a global coaching and consulting firm for women; co-visionary of The Beyond Brilliant Network; and the founder of The S.W.A.G. University—a coaching and personal development initiative designed to disrupt the ordinary and ignite extraordinary growth. Her passion extends into community service as Board Chair of Diamond in the Rough, a youth development nonprofit.

From corporate classrooms in China to conference halls in South Africa, Dr. Dee has shared her voice across the globe, but her mission remains rooted in homegrown truth: *you don't have to wait for permission to lead powerfully.*

When she's not writing, speaking, or mentoring, you'll find her deep in purpose—investing in her family, her community, and her faith. She is a woman of vision, grit, and grace—walking out her calling while championing yours.

I'm the hand on your back pushing you out of your comfort zone into your courage zone. I'll help you cultivate a mindset of courage to achieve success and fulfillment both personally and professionally.

DR. DEYONNE PARKER

To work with Dr. DeYonne "Dee" Parker:

🌐 www.deyonneparker.com

▥ @deyonneparker | #YourSignatureMove

CLIENT TESTIMONIALS

66 ────────────

"In the short time that I've known Dr. Dee, she has made a profound impact on me, my beliefs, and my mindset. She has helped me grow as a writer and leader by encouraging me to face my fears and doubts and tap into the greatness within me. Her book "Your Signature Move" is a powerful catalyst to be bold and courageous in your professional and personal life".

**SHANI AVERY-SCOTT,
WRITER AND LEADER**

──────────── 99

66 ────────────

"Dr. Parker didn't just coach me-she activated me. Her process helped me silence my inner doubts, reclaim my confidence, and walk boldly in my purpose. I'm a better leader, wife and woman because of her guidance."

*CHANEL M.,
CORPORATE EXECUTIVE LEADER*

──────────── 99

"Dr. DeYonne Parker has made a tremendous impact in my life—both personally and professionally. Her wisdom, strategic insight, and unwavering belief in helping women rise with courage have continually transformed the way I think, lead, and live. Through every masterclass, book, journal, and face-to-face encounter, she has challenged me not to settle for being merely comfortable, but to be courageous, confident, and committed to living a life beyond brilliant. Her latest book, Your Signature Move, is no exception. From the very first chapter, I was captivated and convicted. It's more than a book—it's a call to action, a mirror of my untapped potential, and a guide that helped me silence my inner critic and start moving boldly in my purpose. As someone who is both building a business and navigating new levels of leadership, this book came right on time. It reminded me of a powerful truth:" the most defining moments in life don't come from waiting for permission—they come from boldly choosing to make your move. If you've ever hesitated, second-guessed yourself, or played small—Your Signature Move is your wake-up call. Dr. Parker has once again delivered transformational truth wrapped in practical wisdom. And I, for one, am moving differently because of it."

**MONIQUE KELLY,
CORPORATE PROFESSIONAL AND ENTREPRENEUR**